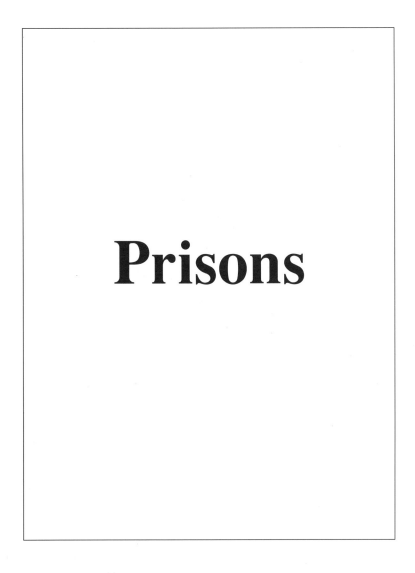

Prisons

Look for these and other books in the Lucent Overview series:

Prisons

by Lois Warburton

LUCENT
B·O·O·K·S

LUCENT Overview Series

LUCENT *Overview Series*

To Renée and Gina,
Daughters of the Heart

Library of Congress Cataloging-in-Publication Data

Warburton, Lois, 1938-
    Prisons / by Lois Warburton.
        p.   cm. — (Lucent overview series)
    Includes bibliographical references and index.
    Summary: Discusses prisons in this country, including their history,
philosophy of punishment, prison conditions, keeping people out of prisons,
prison reform, and the goal of prisons.
    ISBN 1-56006-138-3 (alk. paper)
    1. Prisons—United States—Juvenile literature.   [1. Prisons.]
I. Title. II. Series.
HV9471.W35   1993
365'.973—dc20

                             92-43246
                                  CIP
                                  AC

Copyright © 1993 by Lucent Books, Inc.
P.O. Box 289011, San Diego, CA 92198-9011
Printed in the USA

Contents

Introduction

IN OCTOBER 1991, as winter approached, Vernon Lamarr Clark walked unarmed but determined into a San Diego bank and handed the teller a note. "This is a robbery," said the note. "Give me your cash." Clark took the forty dollars he was handed, told a security guard to call the police, and waited patiently to be arrested.

Clark was neither a bank robber nor mentally disturbed; he was an unemployed iron worker who had been homeless for a year. "I was tired and fed up with sleeping on the streets and picking through Dumpsters for food," he said. He robbed the bank so he would be clothed, fed, and sheltered in prison.

Without hope

Most prisons are crowded, noisy, violent, and thoroughly unpleasant places. They are not the kind of place a person would go voluntarily unless that person was desperate. Clark was desperate. He had no home, no job, and no money. Most critical of all, he had lost all hope of securing a better future through lawful means. Clark's decision to seek out imprisonment is not typical of most offenders, but his hopelessness is. Urban and rural slums throughout the United States are full of desperate people who see no hope of achieving their share of the American Dream

(Opposite page) The setting sun marks the passing of yet another day for those locked inside the walls of a typical American prison.

7

through lawful means. It is they who constitute the majority of our prison population.

The typical prison inmate is a young male between the ages of eighteen and thirty. He is poorly educated; in fact, there is a 40 percent chance that he cannot read. Because of his lack of education and training, he has seldom held a decent job. Nor are there apt to be any decent jobs in the poverty-stricken neighborhood he comes from. Furthermore, fractured families and disintegrating communities do not encourage education, achievement, or self-esteem. Rather, they create a vacuum in which drugs, alcohol, and gangs become a strong attraction.

When he was young, the typical inmate decided he wanted to be like the people he knew who seemed to have made it despite the odds. The pimp in his fancy Cadillac, the drug dealer in his thousand-dollar suit, the gang leader with his power to make others afraid and respectful—they were his role models. Because of these influences, he began getting in trouble with the law as a juvenile and has been imprisoned before adulthood.

During his several prison terms, the inmate may receive some education or perhaps some drug rehabilitation, but when he is released, there still are no decent jobs available and no community support for a new life. Instead, there are his old gang members with their quick money from street crime and their fake, drug-induced hope. So he is right back where he started, trapped in a vicious cycle of poverty, ignorance, unemployment, hopelessness, and crime.

Root causes

Penologists (specialists in penal or prison theory), federal and state lawmakers, and the general public respond to this cycle by spending millions of dollars each year to punish him and the thou-

Southern Michigan State Prison inmates train for jobs in the horticultural industry. Two inmates (right and front) discuss their work with visitors.

sands like him with imprisonment. They keep hoping prisons will act like a magic wand and make crime disappear. If this happened, the expense would make sense. But the odds indicate that the typical inmate will break the law again and return to prison. For him, prison does not break the cycle; it simply becomes part of it.

Because of this, many thinkers have said for years that building more and more prisons is the wrong answer to a rising crime rate. Yes, they say, we must have prisons to protect society from violent, hardened criminals, but prisons will never solve the crime problem. To do that, we must attack the root causes of much crime: poverty, inequality, lack of education, lack of jobs and job skills, the collapse of family and community, and the feelings of hopelessness and helplessness. Studies have shown, for example, that as levels of income and education rise, rates of crime decrease.

No one pretends that eradicating the root causes of crime in the United States would be easy. In fact, there are many who say it cannot be done. Certainly it is impossible to even try without a huge investment of time, energy, and funds. It is really a question of priorities. For two hundred years punishing offenders and building more prisons to hold them has been the priority. As journalist Molly Ivins said in *Progressive* magazine:

Many people who end up in prison have had little education. These prison inmates make use of their time behind bars to further their learning.

> In one of those chilling conjunctions that occasionally make our problems too, too clear, the same day the [Texas House of Representatives] voted to save $206 million by cutting the funds for the pre-kindergarten programs, the House also voted to spend an additional $400 million to build new prisons. Seven out of ten prison inmates are school dropouts. As Representative Wilhelmina Delco of Austin said, "It boggles my mind. The very kids who would profit the most from education are also the ones who all indicators show will be the ones to go to prison." There it is.

1

Punishment to Penitence

PRISONS ARE SO COMMON today that it is easy to believe that these mysterious, walled fortresses have always been a part of human society. But, in fact, prisons as we know them have existed for only about two hundred years. Before that there was little need for prisons. People who broke the law were not punished by being locked up for a period of time. They were punished quickly, often by death or other extremely harsh, physical ways. It was not unusual for the punishment to be held as a public spectacle. Seeing the punishment, it was thought, would act as a deterrent to keep other people from committing the same crime.

Suicide and revenge

Many ancient civilizations, including the Greeks and Romans, did have places where they confined prisoners. But these places were not used the way prisons are used today. For thousands of years most people believed what the third-century Roman legal expert Ulpian said: "A prison ought to be maintained for holding men, not for punishing them." Prisons were used primarily to keep convicted prisoners from escaping

(Opposite page) An early nineteenth-century prison. Prisons were originally established as humane alternatives to the more common punishments of torture and death.

11

In ancient times, prisons served as places of confinement for condemned persons awaiting execution. Those who escaped execution often suffered torture.

before they could be punished. In 450 B.C., for example, the Greeks built a state prison called "the People's Thing" in Athens. It served mainly as a death row where condemned prisoners were expected to commit suicide by drinking a poison called hemlock. Inside one of its rooms the famous Greek philosopher Socrates met just such a death in 399 B.C.

In many ancient cultures criminals were punished not by the state, but through personal revenge, similar to the "eye for an eye" philosophy in the Bible. Other cultures developed official systems of punishment. For example, until they were conquered in 1066, the Angles and the Saxons of England punished offenders by fining them. This system kept tribal members from constantly taking revenge on each other. The fines, called *wergeld* (man-money), were based on a set value assigned to every man and every part of his body. If someone cut another man's hand, he had to pay the victim the established amount. If he cut off the man's hand, he had to pay even more. Anyone who could not pay the *wergeld* was mutilated, enslaved, or killed.

The Norman rulers who conquered the Angles and the Saxons wanted to be in charge of punishing criminals, but they liked the idea of fines. They quickly changed the law so that the fines would be paid to the king instead of to the victims. This meant the kings became responsible for catching criminals and collecting the fines. They soon discovered that most criminals disappeared before the fines were paid. Therefore, in 1154 King Henry II initiated the next step in the use of confinement. He ordered that jails (spelled *gaols* in Great Britain) be built in every English county.

Socrates, surrounded by mournful disciples, awaits the fatal effects of the poison he has drunk in the People's Thing, the ancient prison of Athens.

Languishing in jail

These jails served the same purpose our jails serve today: they detained people who had been accused of crimes until trials could be held to determine their guilt or innocence. Jails are not meant to punish. Prisons are. This is the major difference between jails and prisons.

Although King Henry's jails were not meant to punish, they must have felt like punishment to those held there. Men, women, and children were put into one large, crowded room that was infested with rats and fleas. These vermin caused so many cases of typhoid fever, an infectious and often fatal intestinal disease, that it became known as gaol fever because people believed the jails themselves caused it. Prisoners died five times more often than did free people.

The prisoners were under the charge of a jailer, whose only source of income was what he could collect from them. They had to pay him for food, straw for bedding, and firewood. The rich, who could afford to pay him, were often separated from the poor and allowed to have servants and furniture. The poor had to rely on charity or go without. And everyone had to pay a release fee before they could leave, even if they were found innocent. People who could not pay the fee might languish in jail until they died. These conditions existed in jails for hundreds of years.

Saving souls

The kings and jailers cared only about collecting their fees. They were not interested in the criminals' motives or whether they were sorry for

Early English jails were so crowded, unsanitary, and vermin-infested that infectious diseases claimed the lives of many inmates before they could go to trial.

what they had done. The Roman Catholic church, however, did care, for it wanted to save souls. From this caring developed the idea of rehabilitation, reforming criminals so they would stop committing crimes.

By the twelfth century the church had its own law courts, which were based on the principle of repentance. These courts, open only to Roman Catholics, were far more lenient than the civil courts. The church considered it un-Christian to execute or physically punish a person who had repented and asked God's forgiveness. Convicted criminals were given acts of repentance as punishment. They might be sentenced to take a pilgrimage to a religious shrine or fast on bread and water or take cold baths.

There were some people, however, whom the church considered untrustworthy. To ensure that these people obeyed the court's orders, they were confined to monasteries where the monks supervised their acts of repentance. Thus, the church introduced the idea that criminals could be rehabilitated through confinement and repentance, without using confinement as punishment.

In the sixteenth century the Roman Catholic church was banished from England by King Henry VIII. He was angry because the pope would not allow him to divorce his queen and remarry, so he established himself as the head of a new English church, the Anglican church. The Roman Catholic church court disappeared, but some reformers retained the notion of rehabilitating criminals through certain types of confinement and soon saw a need to put it into practice.

King Henry VIII banished the Roman Catholic church from England in the sixteenth century. However, the English legal system maintained the church's practice of helping criminals repent their crimes.

Harsh penalties

Sixteenth-century England was emerging into the modern world and undergoing many economic changes. Feudalism was breaking down.

Feudalism was a system whereby peasants farmed a nobleman's land in return for a home and their lord's protection. Unable to afford this system any longer, nobles forced the peasants off their land. Homeless and destitute, many families wandered into the cities to become part of the increasing population of urban poor. These thousands of vagabonds, as they were called, were criminals, for to be homeless and unemployed was then a crime. Indeed, many turned to theft and begging to survive.

Harsh penalties were passed to control vagabondage. Vagabonds over the age of fourteen, for instance, were "grievously whipped and burned through the gristle of the right ear with a hot iron." These penalties did not solve the problem. The homeless poor had only one lawful alternative, England's workhouses, also known as poorhouses. Because of a growing humane attitude toward the poor, workhouses had been established to house and provide employment for the old, sick, and destitute. But there were too few workhouses and too many vagabonds.

Houses of correction

In 1557 King Edward VI established the first house of correction in an abandoned palace. The original purpose of the Bridewell house of correction was to get "the lewd and idle" off the streets by confining them. But the idea of reform was not forgotten. In the belief that poverty was a vice no better than thievery, prison officials forced inmates to work under strict discipline. Spinning cloth and baking bread was meant to help vagabonds overcome their "idle" ways. This enforced labor was considered an enlightened approach to vagabondage and introduced the idea of rehabilitation through hard work, as well as repentance.

King Edward VI established England's first house of correction in 1557.

Parliament, the English governing body, considered the house of correction such a good idea that it passed a law in 1576 calling for Bridewells, as they all came to be called, in every county. In theory Bridewells were humane institutions. They gave the homeless housing and employment, even though it was at the price of their freedom. In practice, however, both Bridewells and workhouses were soon filled with all types of misfits: criminals, orphans, runaways, mentally disabled, and insane. In the end there was no difference between the two institutions. They were both overcrowded and poorly managed. Inmates went hungry and were treated cruelly. Soon most Bridewells and workhouses were no better than the jails.

Inmates of houses of correction often fared better in the rest of Europe, where the idea of rehabilitation through penitence and work spread rapidly. In 1704 the Hospice of San Michele was established in Rome by Pope Clement XI, with the goal of teaching wayward boys to work, pray, and repent. Over the door of the hospice was the

The Bridewell, an abandoned English palace, became a house of correction in 1557. Bridewell thereafter became the popular term for the correctional institutions established in every English county.

inscription: "It is insufficient to restrain the wicked by punishment unless you render them virtuous by corrective discipline." In Ghent, Belgium, a successful workhouse with the same goals was begun by Jean Jacques Vilain in 1771. Vilain was the first administrator to separate women and children from men, and serious offenders from lesser ones. The inmates lived in individual cells and were forbidden to talk to each other, because Vilain believed repentance would come faster in isolation and silence.

Extreme cruelty

Despite the fact that the eighteenth century is known as the Age of Enlightenment for its humanitarian advances, physical mutilation and death continued to be the most common forms of punishment. In his book *Discipline and Punish*, for example, Michel Foucault quotes from an account of the execution of a Frenchman named Damiens. In 1757 Damiens was condemned to be

> taken and conveyed in a cart, wearing nothing but a shirt, holding a torch of burning wax weighing two pounds . . . to [a public square in front of the church], where, on a scaffold that will be erected there, the flesh will be torn from his breasts, arms, thighs and calves with red-hot pincers, his right hand, holding the knife with which he committed the [murder], burnt with sulphur, and, on those places where the flesh will be torn away, poured molten lead, boiling oil, burning resin, wax and sulphur melted together and then his body drawn and quartered by four horses and his limbs and body consumed by fire, reduced to ashes and his ashes thrown to the winds.

Such extreme cruelty prompted reformers to look for alternate punishments, at least for minor crimes. For example, between 1732 and 1776, between 50,000 and 100,000 English convicts were banished to the British colonies in America for life. In 1776 the American Revolution ended that program. Faced with a growing number of convicts they did not know what to do with, the English began to confine more and more of them in jails. Soon the jails were more crowded and inhumane than ever.

These conditions prompted the English to take a closer look at their jails and Bridewells. In 1773 an Englishman named John Howard became interested in jail reform and began visiting jails throughout England and eventually throughout Europe. Conditions in England's jails and Bridewells appalled him, but in Europe he found some institutions he admired. Among them were the workhouses set up by Pope Clement and Vilain. Howard's goal became the introduction of their reforms to England's jails.

Making people sorry

In 1777 Howard wrote a book entitled *The State of Prisons in England and Wales*. In it he advocated building prisons with individual cells for prisoners, adequate food, and medical care. He called for sanitary, humane conditions and, especially, a program of isolation and silence that encouraged inmates to repent. He called these prisons penitentiaries, thereby introducing the word into our language. *Penitentiary* means, literally, an institution that makes people sorry.

In 1779 Howard talked Parliament into passing the Penitentiary Act. It called for four main reforms: the building of two secure, sanitary penitentiaries with individual cells; systematic inspection of the prisons to ensure their proper operation; the end of fees for basic services; and a regime of silence and work that promoted rehabilitation through repentance. The act makes it clear that imprisonment had finally been accepted as a proper punishment for some crimes and that

Parliament believed prisons would serve to rehabilitate criminals and deter crime. If criminals,
the law states,

> were ordered to solitary imprisonment, accompa-
> nied by well-regulated labour and religious in-
> struction, it might be the means . . . not only of de-
> terring others from the commission of like crimes
> but also of reforming the individuals.

Howard was appointed supervisor of buildings
for the two proposed penitentiaries, but he never
saw them built. After a year of listening to arguments over where the first one should be located,
Howard resigned. Parliament did not deal with
the problem of prisons again for twelve years.
Howard died in 1790 from gaol fever, which he
caught during a visit to a Russian prison. But his
work, and that of Vilain and other eighteenth-cen-
tury reformers, formed the foundations of modern
penal theory. The word *penal* refers to anything
relating to punishment.

A model penitentiary

It was in the United States that Howard's reforms first came to fruition. The American penal
system was based on the one in England. The
jails here were just as deplorable, and the punishments just as cruel. In Pennsylvania the Quakers,
a religious group that believes in nonviolence and
salvation, were the only colonists who tried to
treat criminals humanely. After the United States
became independent the Quakers led the way in
prison reform.

Influenced by Howard's work, the Pennsylvania legislature voted in 1790 to create a
model penitentiary in a wing of Philadelphia's
Walnut Street Jail. It was the first true prison and
was dedicated to punishment by confinement and
rehabilitation by repentance. Walnut Street fea-
tured several reforms. Inmates were each given a

determinate sentence, a sentence of a specific length, so they knew when they would be released. They did not pay fees because their upkeep was paid by the state. And serious offenders were separated from lesser offenders.

The latter slept in large dormitories and worked at a craft such as shoemaking or tailoring. Hardened criminals, on the other hand, were put in solitary confinement without work so that they might repent more quickly by having all their time to reflect on their crimes. After a time, however, it became apparent that idle isolation caused mental illness rather than repentance. Thereafter, the isolated criminals were also given work, as well as moral and religious instruction.

By 1818 Walnut Street was overcrowded, and the Pennsylvania legislature voted to build two new, giant penitentiaries: Western Penitentiary in Pittsburgh and Eastern Penitentiary in Philadelphia. Eastern Penitentiary was also called Cherry Hill because it was built in an old cherry orchard.

A wing of Philadelphia's Walnut Street Jail was the site of a penitentiary modeled on John Howard's reforms. It became the world's first true prison.

Cherry Hill was run on the principle of solitary confinement developed at Walnut Street. It was the model for what became known as the Pennsylvania system, or separate system. At no time were the inmates allowed to leave their cells or private exercise yards. They never saw or talked to another inmate—they were even brought into the prison blindfolded. They worked, ate, and slept alone for the duration of their determinate sentences.

Silence and work

Many people thought total isolation was cruel and unusual punishment. When English author Charles Dickens, an avid social reformer, visited Cherry Hill, he wrote: "Very few men are capable of estimating the immense amount of torture and agony which this dreadful punishment, prolonged for years, inflicts upon sufferers." But others were enthusiastic about the system, and a number of states operated their penitentiaries along similar lines.

Auburn State Prison in New York was one of them. But in the program's first year five inmates died, one went insane, and twenty-six others became so disturbed that they were released. A new system, called the Auburn system, or silent system, was put into effect. Inmates lived in individual cells, but they worked and ate together. The catch was that they had to do everything in total silence. Even attempting nonverbal communication with a fellow prisoner was punished by flogging.

Many arguments arose about which system was better, but actually the systems were very similar. Both were based on the beliefs that imprisonment was the best punishment for criminals and that prisons would deter crime. Both advocated that silence, obedience, and hard work were the keys to penitence, and hence to rehabilitation.

Charles Dickens's writings inspired many social reforms in England. He believed the nineteenth-century policy of isolation adopted by American penitentiaries was inhumane.

But the main similarity between the two systems was that neither of them worked. The silence and solitary confinement damaged prisoners' mental health. Even determinate sentencing contributed to the failure of the systems. Since good behavior would not get them released earlier, inmates had no incentive to behave well or work hard.

Making matters worse

To make matters worse, the purpose of the hard work forced on the inmates switched from rehabilitation to bringing in money to help support the prisons. Because wardens were judged on how much their prisoners produced, they instituted harsh rules to make the prisoners work hard. In an attempt to control the prisoners and enforce the harsh rules, guards became increasingly cruel.

Furthermore, it became evident that neither system was deterring crime and that silence and separation were not producing penitence or rehabilitation. Crime and recidivism (when a released prisoner commits more crime) continued to rise. As a result, prisons became overcrowded, and cells built for one person soon held two. Under these conditions many wardens forgot about rehabilitation entirely and concentrated on maintaining control.

In the end, the Auburn system was judged best because its prisoners, working in groups, produced more goods and brought more money to the penitentiaries than did the Pennsylvania system. But by the 1850s it did not matter. Americans had decided their prisons were not working. The New York Prison Commission reported in 1852 that prolonged imprisonment "destroys the better faculties [abilities] of the soul."

2

Penitence to Punishment

THE FAILURE OF nineteenth-century penitentiaries could be read in the prison statistics. In 1850 they held seven thousand prisoners; by 1870 that figure had jumped to thirty-three thousand. But prison administrators did not need statistics to tell them prisons were in trouble. They lived with the problems every day. In 1870 they decided to do something about it.

In that year a group of penologists met in Cincinnati, Ohio, to talk about penal reform. This meeting was the birth of the professional association of penologists now called the American Correctional Association. When Zebulon Brockway, warden of the Detroit House of Correction, said at the meeting that the goal of prisons should be "the protection of society by the prevention of crime, and reformation of criminals," he was speaking for most of those present. Reformation, meaning reform or rehabilitation, became the new hope for the success of incarceration. The idea of penitence was abandoned.

Reforms

The penologists left the meeting determined to reform the penal system. The main methods they

(Opposite page) A typical cell block in a modern state prison. Modern prisons emphasize punishment, although rehabilitation is also a goal.

25

intended to use came from the work of two men: Capt. Alexander Maconochie and Walter Crofton. Maconochie was the director of an English penal colony on Norfolk Island in Australia from 1840 to 1844. Before he had arrived Norfolk was so notoriously inhumane that some convicted criminals, fearing incarceration there, drowned themselves. Maconochie introduced a number of reforms, among them the indeterminate sentence, a sentence without a definite release date. Prisoners had to win their freedom by earning a set number of credits for hard work and good behavior. The harder they worked and the better they behaved, the faster they earned their credits. "When a man keeps the key to his own prison," Maconochie wrote, "he is soon persuaded to fit it to the lock."

Earning freedom

Walter Crofton, one of the men who ran Ireland's prisons, adapted many of Maconochie's ideas for use in Ireland during the 1850s. After first spending nine months in solitary confinement, Irish convicts earned their way to freedom through a five-step program. When they were released, they were given a "ticket of release." If they got into any trouble in the next ten years, the ticket was revoked, and they were returned to prison. This ticket of release was the first system of parole, or conditional release.

Along with indeterminate sentences and parole, American reformers wanted convicts to receive education, especially vocational education, which would teach them a trade they could pursue after their release. According to Zebulon Brockway, education was the key to reform:

> The effect of education is reformatory, for it tends to dissipate poverty by imparting intelligence sufficient to conduct ordinary affairs, and puts into

the mind, necessarily, habits of punctuality, method and perseverance. . . . If culture, then, has a refining influence, it is only necessary to carry it far enough, in combination always with due religious agencies, to cultivate the criminal out of his criminality, and to constitute him a reformed man.

The reformatory at Elmira, New York, incorporated the latest ideas on reform and rehabilitation for inmates. It failed nevertheless.

A new type of prison

In 1876 Brockway got the chance to put these ideas into practice. In that year the New York legislature voted to open a new type of prison, a reformatory, in Elmira, New York. It was solely for males ages sixteen to thirty, perhaps because men over thirty did not seem good prospects for reformation.

Brockway not only used indeterminate sentences, parole, and job training at Elmira, but he also established a number of rehabilitation programs that included a library, a glee club, an athletic field, and a gym. The inmates participated in military drill and religious instruction and published a newspaper. It seemed like a place that could not fail. Yet it did, and so did all the other reformatories built in the United States.

One of the reasons for failure was the indeterminate sentence. Inmates soon learned that, by doing the right things and saying what wardens and parole boards wanted to hear, they could fake their reform and beat the system. Once out on parole they often returned to crime.

Another reason for failure was the lack of funds. There was seldom enough money to institute and operate effective programs. Unable to hire good vocational teachers, reformatories had to use guards to teach courses. The guards were often more interested in discipline than in teaching and made the classes feel like punishment to the inmates. In fact, no matter how hard Brockway and other reformers tried, the inmates, guards, and many administrators and members of the general public saw punishment as the purpose of all penal institutions. Before long reformatories became junior prisons with many of the same problems.

Inmates at the Minnesota State Prison in Stillwater mill around the prison yard during an hour of recreation that was part of their regimen in the 1950s.

Although reformatories were used well into the twentieth century, it was clear by 1900 that they did not work. Their recidivism rate was no better than that of the penitentiaries, and in 1900 there were fifty-seven thousand people in American penal institutions. However, reformatories did leave a lasting legacy. They had, for instance, introduced education as a necessary element of reform. They had made the indeterminate sentence and parole part of American penology. And they brought about some permanent changes in the way prisons are designed and organized.

Leading the way

For instance, reformatories had shown that it was good policy to separate young offenders from hardened criminals. They had also shown that not all offenders needed to be treated in the traditional, harsh manner. This knowledge led to classifying offenders into categories so that each type of offender could be housed in a separate institution and treated differently. This classification led to the first reformatory solely for women, which was built in Massachusetts in 1877.

Reformatories also led to permanent changes in prison architecture by initiating theories about minimum and maximum security. Hardened criminals had to be guarded carefully in maximum security behind high walls. But there was no need to build an expensive, walled fortress to hold lesser offenders who could be trusted not to escape. They could be held in less fortified, minimum-security prisons, where they had more freedom and could learn personal responsibility. Minimum security worked so well for certain types of offenders that, in 1916, Washington, D.C., built its Lorton, Virginia, reformatory without any walls at all.

But because reformatories were ineffective at

Handcuffed to the bars of his cell, an inmate endures the punishment of solitary confinement in a state reformatory.

Inmates work in a prison twine factory in 1914. Prison labor was cheap for contractors and helped reduce costs for prisons.

rehabilitating criminals, reformers seeking new answers to penal problems at the turn of the century decided to update an old idea. They developed industrial prisons and put the inmates to work earning money for the state. Prison populations were growing and becoming a financial burden to the states. Convict labor was seen as a way to turn that around and make a profit. Since harsh discipline seemed the best way to keep the prisoners well behaved and productive, punishment and hard labor again became the key words.

Some states, particularly in the South, leased their prisoners cheaply to private contractors who were building roads and railroads and running mines and farms. The contractors were responsible for housing, feeding, and clothing the prisoners. This was seldom done in a humane way, for the contractors cared only about making a profit. The prisoners labored in chain gangs, linked together with iron chains, and were often worked to death. Those who tried to escape were shot.

Most states, however, kept convicts under their direct control by turning their prisons into facto-

Convicts were cooped up in a cell-on-wheels while working on chain gangs constructing roads in early twentieth-century California.

ries. Private manufacturers paid the states to have their products made by the inmates inside the prison. The silent system was abolished, and the inmates were often paid a small wage as incentive to work hard, but, in general, life in prison became even harsher.

By 1930 the prison population had grown to 148,000. Much of this growth came from a rise in crime due partly to unemployment after World War I. Convictions stemming from the Volstead Act of 1918, which made illegal the manufacture and sale of alcohol, also increased the number of prisoners. Thirty-one new prisons and seven reformatories had been built between 1900 and 1925, but overcrowding was a bigger problem than ever. Up to four convicts were put in a cell that measured, perhaps, six by eight feet. Rehabilitation, including educational, recreational, and religious programs, was virtually nonexistent. Under these conditions there was little chance an inmate would be reformed.

Convict labor

Despite the fact that punishment and hard labor were not deterring crime or reforming prisoners, the industrial system might have continued if the states had continued making a profit. By the 1930s, however, they no longer were. This was primarily due to the fact that other manufacturers and the labor organizations believed that competition from prison-manufactured goods was unfair. Because they were made with cheap convict labor, the products could be sold at lower prices. After the Great Depression hit in 1929, the public also began complaining, because convicts were being paid when law-abiding citizens could not find jobs. In response most states passed laws prohibiting the sale of prison-made goods that competed with goods made elsewhere.

Prisoners in this early twentieth-century state prison slept in an open dormitory. On the floor below was the prison factory where they worked during the day.

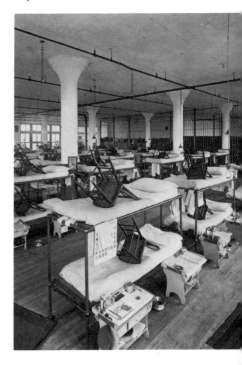

These laws signaled the end of the industrial prisons and the end of forced hard labor for prisoners in most states, but they did not eliminate prison-industry programs altogether. Some inmates, particularly those in the federal prisons, are still taught trades through the production of noncompetitive goods. Other inmates perform maintenance and clerical jobs for the prisons themselves. Still others work at minimal wages for outside firms, performing such tasks as computer data entry and making airline reservations. This work contributes to the financial independence of the inmates after their release and to the prisons' budgets, but it is no longer the mainstay of the prison system.

A psychological cure

In the 1930s, with the industrial model failing, penologists once again began searching for a more effective way to solve penal problems. This time they found their answer in the new science of psychology. Psychology had developed as a profession after World War I to treat soldiers who had emotional problems as a result of the horrors of war. Soon it was seen as a way for the states to deal with social problems such as crime and prisons.

Psychologists maintained that people committed crime not because they were evil, but because they were sick. Their behavior was caused by biological or psychological conditions that could be cured through treatment. Psychiatrist Karl Menninger summed up this theory in his book, *The Crime of Punishment*, saying that criminal acts are "signals of distress, signals of failure . . . the spasms of struggles and convulsions of a . . . human being trying to make it in our complex society with inadequate equipment and inadequate preparation."

Thus began the so-called medical model of

penology, which lasted until about 1970. This form of rehabilitation was first adopted by the new federal Bureau of Prisons when it was created in 1930 to maintain federal prisons for "the safe-keeping, care, protection, instruction and discipline of all persons charged or convicted of offenses against the United States." Many states soon followed suit.

Therapeutic communities

Prisons, also called correctional centers, became therapeutic communities that attempted to give convicts the proper treatment. Prisoners were tested and interviewed so that they could be classified according to type of illness. Then they were given individual courses of treatment designed to cure them. They not only received education and job training, they were also assigned to all types of therapy programs.

Malcolm Braly, a former convict, describes in his book *False Starts* what it was like to be a prisoner during this period.

> We quickly learned we were expected to view this journey through prison as a quest, and the object of our quest was to discover our problem. It was assumed we were here because of psychological problems, and our task now, by which we could expect to be judged, was to isolate and come to terms with them. Boys who had stolen cars were thought to be acting out a symbolic return to the womb and once they had been helped to understand their true motivation and recognize its utter futility they would be free of the compulsion. . . . And no matter what your private opinion, when the . . . [parole board] asked in tones of high seriousness if you had come to grips with your problem, you were willing to concede you might have a problem even if you had to invent one on the spot.

Now that punishment was unpopular and treatment was favored, prison was expected to provide a totally humane environment. The prison

Inmates, some completely stripped of clothes, are made to lie on the ground while waiting to be searched at New York's Attica State Prison after inmates rioted.

that opened in Attica, New York, in 1931 was a prime example. According to the August 2, 1931, issue of the *New York Times*,

> New York State will have an answer to charges of inhuman penal conditions when the new New York State Prison opens at Attica . . . with its full quota of 2,000 convicts. Said to be the last word in modern prison construction, the new unit . . . will do away with such traditions as convict bunks, mess hall lockstep [synchronized activity], bull pens [group cells], and even locks and keys.

> In their place will be beds with springs and mattresses, a cafeteria with food under glass, recreation rooms and an automatic signal system by which convicts will notify guards of their presence in their cells. Doors will be operated by compressed air, sunlight will stream into cells and every prisoner will have an individual radio.

Forty years later, in 1971, Attica was the scene of perhaps the most famous riot in prison history. On September 9, armed with clubs, rakes, and knives, about thirteen hundred inmates overpowered the guards, took forty-three hostages, and held the prison for four days. They demanded amnesty—"freedom for all and from all physical, mental and legal reprisal"—as well as twenty-eight changes, such as better medical care, better food, more minority guards, and the end of censorship of their mail. Although many officials felt some of the demands were reasonable, they were not willing to be forced into agreement by violence. On September 13, state troopers stormed the yard where the prisoners were gathered and opened fire. Four minutes later, nine hostages and twenty-nine inmates were dead, three hostages and eighty-five inmates were wounded, and the riot was over.

Failure and rebuilding

Something had gone terribly wrong. Attica was only one of many prison riots between 1950 and 1971. The American Correctional Association investigated these riots and reported the following causes: overcrowding, poor management, lack of funds, poorly trained and unmotivated personnel, enforced idleness among prisoners, lack of rehabilitation programs, and unwise sentencing and parole practices.

Strained relations between the races—a festering issue outside the walls as well—also contributed to the problems inside the prisons. Racially motivated violence, between prisoners and guards and between prisoners of different races, added to the tension. Prison managers tried to keep the tension under control by curtailing educational, vocational, and other rehabilitation programs. As conditions in prison worsened, inmates built up more and more resentment. When they tried to speak out, no one listened. It took riots to make prison managers and the public take notice and listen.

The aftermath of the 1971 Attica riot. Rebelling prisoners held hostages for four days in this exercise yard.

By the time of the Attica riot in 1971, many Americans could recognize the validity of many of the complaints being made by the 196,000 inmates in the country's prisons. Civil rights activists, including lawyers and judges, joined with the inmates in fighting to ensure the inmates' basic rights for decent treatment and living conditions. At Attica, for example, to relieve the crowding some inmates were transferred to other prisons. Furthermore, all inmates were given periodic medical examinations to safeguard against unreported beatings. Diets were improved and additional bathing facilities were provided.

New freedoms

Throughout the country the medical model died quickly as it was replaced by a renewed effort at rehabilitation through prison reform. Many rules were relaxed. Prisoners were allowed to wear their own clothing, keep many personal possessions in their cells, and meet directly with friends and family instead of talking to them from behind a barred partition. Mail was no longer censored. Minority guards were recruited. New work and recreational programs were developed so inmates would not have to spend their days in idleness. The increasing number of inmates with drug problems were offered drug rehabilitation programs. Illiterate inmates were offered basic education courses. Inmates were encouraged to take advantage of sports activities and libraries. Soon some new penal institutions looked more like college campuses than traditional prisons.

These new freedoms made prison management more difficult. Contact visits made it easy for friends and family to smuggle in drugs and other contraband to the prisoners. Inmates found it easier to manufacture weapons, and murders inside prisons increased, as did rape and theft. At the

Except for the barbed-wire fence, this exercise yard at a modern state prison in North Carolina might be mistaken for a school yard. Present-day convicts enjoy greater freedoms than the prisoners of days past.

same time, the recidivism rate remained high and the crime rate in society rose. By 1980 there were 321,000 people in American prisons.

"Nothing works"

Many people began to doubt that prisons could rehabilitate convicts. As proof they began to quote a study done in 1974 by Robert Martinson at the City University of New York. He and his colleagues reviewed 231 studies of rehabilitation programs published between 1945 and 1967. The programs included educational and vocational training, various forms of therapy, medical treatment, drug rehabilitation, and parole, among others. Using such signs of rehabilitation as lack of recidivism, vocational success, educational achievement, adjustment to prison, and personality and attitude change, each study had compared the results for offenders who attended its program with those of offenders who did not. "With few and isolated exceptions," Martinson found, "the rehabilitative efforts that have been reported so far have had no appreciable effect on recidivism." This finding brought a quick end to the 1970s rehabilitation model.

When the media reported Martinson's study, it invented the catchphrase for penology in 1980: "nothing works." If prisons cannot rehabilitate inmates, many people decided, then prisons should concentrate on punishment.

3

Prisons Today

DESPITE THE DISAPPOINTING findings of the 1970s, social activists and most penologists have not given up on rehabilitative efforts behind bars. Today's prisons combine the punishment of imprisonment with rehabilitation.

Some convicts respond to this combination and turn their lives around. Donald V. Stanley is a good example. While serving four years in a California prison for serious juvenile offenses, Stanley earned a community college degree and diligently worked at his prison job as an airline reservations agent. When he was paroled at age twenty-one Stanley went to work for TWA full-time. "I'm living proof," Stanley told *Business Week*, "that it's worth giving people a second chance."

Crowded, noisy, violent

Unfortunately, most convicts do not respond to help the way Stanley did. Prisons, for the most part, have been unable to deter and control crime while at the same time preparing offenders for a new life outside the walls. Part of the difficulty in achieving these goals has been conditions within the prisons themselves. Many of the nation's nearly thirteen hundred prisons are overcrowded, noisy, and violent.

Prison overcrowding has long been a problem,

(Opposite page) Inmates line up outside their cells for a daily head count. Overcrowding remains one of the greatest problems in today's prisons.

39

but today it has reached gigantic proportions. In California, for example, prisons have routinely been operating at 175 percent of their capacity. That means there are 175 prisoners for every one hundred prison beds the state has available. In 1991 there were 118,000 more inmates in the United States than there were prison beds.

This situation can be tied, experts contend, to the "get tough on crime" attitude that found a voice in the late 1970s. That attitude was a reaction to a significant increase in violent street crime, that is, such highly visible crimes as robberies, muggings, rapes, gang wars, and drug deals. People began to fear not only for their possessions, but also for their personal safety. With this fear came the desire to punish the offenders and get them off the streets for a long time. At least while they were in prison, their violence could not be directed at honest members of society. So the public demanded that something be done.

"Just deserts"

Penologists and government officials responded to this demand by adopting a new model for imprisonment. They called it "just deserts," and it is still in force today. The theory behind just deserts is really a very old idea. It states that people who infringe on other people's rights by breaking the law deserve punishment and that the severity of the punishment should match the severity of the crime. In other words, prisons should punish, and punishment should provide justice for both victim and offender.

Out of the get-tough-on-crime era arose the nation's War on Drugs. This so-called war is intended to rid the streets of drug dealers and users whose actions have been viewed as a major cause of violent crime. During this period arrests have risen sharply. Judges have handed down longer,

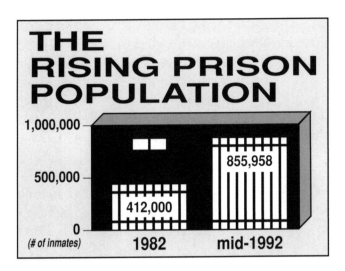

THE RISING PRISON POPULATION

1,000,000

500,000

855,958

412,000

0

(# of inmates) 1982 mid-1992

tougher sentences. States returned to determinate sentencing in an effort to keep offenders in prison for their full terms. In addition, many states passed mandatory sentences for violent crimes, repeat offenders, and drug violations. A mandatory sentence stipulates the minimum amount of time that must be served for a particular offense.

The War on Drugs has not eliminated drug-related or other crime but has succeeded in filling up the nation's prisons. By 1982 American prisons held 412,000 inmates, a leap of 91,000 in only two years. By mid-1992 that figure had grown to an astounding 855,958. At this rate, say experts, half of America will be behind bars in the year 2050. Despite these figures, despite everything the federal government, state legislators, courts, and police do, street crime has continued to rise. In 1991, 1.9 million violent crimes were reported—a 45 percent increase since 1982. Instead of making the streets safer, just deserts has made prisons dangerously overcrowded.

Overcrowding puts a tremendous strain on the entire prison system. To find beds for the additional prisoners, prison managers have had to become very good at improvising. "To cope with an

A prison in Huntsville, Texas, copes with overcrowding by using temporary structures.

influx of almost 3,000 inmates over the summer," the *New York Times* reported on June 3, 1989, "New York State will begin housing prisoners in gymnasiums starting next week. . . ." In Michigan prefabricated housing was erected. In Florida it was tents. Hundreds of prisoners sleep on the floor in corridors, recreational rooms, barber shops, and offices.

"This is the everyday world for us," said Connecticut correction commissioner Lawrence R. Meachum. "It's a world where people have no place to keep their belongings, where sewage systems back up, where everything is fast-tracked to deal with numbers, not quality. We just can't absorb the growth."

To take advantage of every available bed, prison systems have had to change. The best of the worst prisoners in maximum security must be sent to less crowded medium- or even minimum-security prisons. This leaves maximum-security facilities with only the most hardened criminals,

In 1989 some prisoners in the New York penal system were housed in gymnasiums because state correctional facilities were so overcrowded.

complicating security and control at those prisons. It also means that it is no longer possible, in many cases, to separate hardened criminals from lesser offenders at the prisons with less security. This situation threatens the safety and welfare of lesser offenders and makes the job of the prison manager even more difficult.

Overcrowding also strains the physical capacity of prison buildings and infrastructure. Plumbing, heating, and electrical systems fail periodically from overuse. Buildings, too, eventually fall apart. When crumbling walls and collapsing ceilings have to be repaired, inmates are forced into even tighter quarters. All of this, plus the additional food, equipment, and services needed, puts pressure on prison budgets.

An inmate in a Colorado prison peers out of a dark cell. Overcrowding taxes prisons' power supplies, as well as funding and most other physical resources.

A violent reality

Overcrowding is trouble enough. What makes it worse is that it compounds other problems. Violence is one. Violence has always been a part of prison life. Many experts think that violence is the natural result of a prison environment. They point out that prisons are full of people who are there precisely because of their violent actions. Incarceration does not change this fact. When violent people are locked up, experts say, they are likely to be angry and strike out at those around them.

Inmate violence has touched guards and prisoners alike. Overcrowding has only made it worse. In 1990, the last year for which statistics are currently available, inmates committed 12,189 assaults (such as beatings and rapes) on other inmates, and 5,664 on prison staff. They murdered 54 other inmates and 2 guards. In all, there were 160 violent deaths (including 5 inmates killed by prison staff) and 101 suicides.

Because of this violence, many inmates live in fear. To protect themselves, they join prison gangs, where there is safety and strength in numbers. The gangs, in turn, prey upon the weak. This is a good example of how prisons criminalize inmates, that is, turn them into harder criminals than they were when they entered. Criminalization has always been a common result of imprisonment and is one of the factors that has kept recidivism high.

Gangs

Gangs in prisons operate like gangs on the street. They often form along racial lines, so violence frequently pits one race against another. Gang activity is responsible for a high percentage of prison violence, just as it is responsible for a high percentage of street violence. Organized and powerful, some prison gangs develop elaborate networks of extortion, drug trafficking, prostitution, and contract murder behind prison walls. *Newsweek* quoted Philadelphia deputy district attorney Odell Guyton on this topic: "Every kind of criminal activity that occurs outside also occurs inside the prison—and it is generally more profitable inside."

Much of the prison gangs' activities revolve around drugs. Drugs are an obvious way to bankroll gang operations, especially because prisons are full of drug users caught in the War on Drugs. Estimates of the number of inmates caught in that war range from 40 to 90 percent of America's prison population. The drug buying is arranged by the gangs' contacts on the outside, and the drugs are smuggled into the prison, usually by friends or relatives. Drugs have arrived in prison stuffed into book bindings and babies' diapers. They have been hidden in the visitors' washroom, which a prisoner promptly "cleans," or they are flushed down a toilet to prisoners waiting at the prison's sewage treatment plant.

Prison guards, now usually called correctional officers, know what is going on but are often powerless to stop it. When Nolan McCool, an officer at the Huntsville, Texas, state prison was asked if he had ever stopped a gang member from murdering another inmate, he replied:

> If the opportunity exists, they're going to make the hit. If you tell him, "Put that knife down," he'll look up at you and say, "I ain't through yet." These people are serious. If they don't make this hit, they'll become the person to get hit. So it may be a week or a month or a year . . . but that hit is on.

The rapid increase in numbers of prisoners that has led to severe overcrowding is seldom matched by a proportionate increase in correctional offi-

Inmates at Walpole State Prison in Massachusetts are searched for weapons following a gang-related riot there in 1989.

cers. That means there is often less supervision at a time when more is needed. Officers, asked to work long hours of overtime in an explosive atmosphere, are also under great stress. "It's a lot more dangerous job than it used to be," said Connecticut guard William Stark. "All you want to do is do your shift and get out alive or unhurt."

Drugs and health

Some correctional officers, however, do more than that. They become part of the corruption inside their workplaces. For instance, in Pennsylvania in 1988, at least one hundred guards were arrested and charged with such crimes as smuggling drugs, money, and weapons into prison; helping dangerous inmates to escape; and taking bribes to turn one unit of a prison into a social

REFORMATORY DEFORMATORY

club for reputed mobsters. Fortunately, however, these guards are the exception. The majority are honest people who know that smuggling drugs into prison, for example, will only make their jobs more difficult.

Drugs in prison create an unsafe environment and reduce the effectiveness of educational and drug rehabilitation programs. They also facilitate the spread of diseases such as AIDS (acquired immunodeficiency syndrome) and tuberculosis, a lung disease that is spread in droplets transmitted through the air by coughing. In fact, the increase of these two diseases in prisons is a grave concern to prison officials.

By 1991 officials in New Jersey estimated that 30 to 40 percent of the state's inmates were HIV-positive. (HIV stands for human immunodeficiency virus, a virus that weakens the immune system and causes AIDS.) In one Florida county 50 percent of the inmates who volunteered to be tested were HIV-positive. AIDS was the leading cause of death in New York state prisons, and an estimated nine thousand of the state's fifty-four thousand prisoners were HIV-positive. In late 1991, a new health concern surfaced. Twenty-eight New York prisoners with AIDS and one correctional officer with cancer died after they caught a new drug-resistant type of tuberculosis.

AIDS

Many of the inmates with AIDS, HIV, and tuberculosis were already infected when they arrived in prison. This situation is to be expected when a high percentage of inmates are in prison for drug involvement, since drug users are among those most prone to these diseases. But the prevalence of drugs inside prison, where new needles are scarce and sterilization methods are primitive, facilitates the spread of AIDS. "With the amount

Some prisons isolate HIV-infected inmates, which only adds further stress to their lives. Such inmates have dubbed their isolation units the new death rows.

of needle-sharing that goes on, we are sitting on top of a powder keg," says Doug Nelson, director of the Milwaukee AIDS Project. Since AIDS is also spread by homosexual sex, the frequency of same-sex rape in prisons is a major factor in the spread of this disease.

Overcrowded prison conditions increase the inmates' exposure to infectious diseases such as tuberculosis, which are spread through the air. HIV- and AIDS-infected prisoners are not able to fight these diseases off, as the twenty-eight deaths in New York make evident. Budget problems due to overcrowding also may mean that proper nutrition and experimental treatments are not available. In fact, it sometimes means that medical treatment of any type is inadequate. As crowding increases, heavy demands are put on the prison medical staff at a time when there is no money to hire additional personnel.

"Having AIDS in prison is an endless vigil to insure that you receive the medications and treatment that you need," one inmate with AIDS wrote to the National Commission on AIDS.

> It is dealing with medical personnel who get a thrill out of putting your life and well-being in jeopardy by revealing in sadistic and sinister ways that you are one of the "accused." It is being subject to assaults and "burn-outs" (having your cell set on fire) by other prisoners. It is living with a debilitating fear that someone will find out that you're dying of AIDS and kick you. [Dying of AIDS in prison] is a horrible way to die.

Many prisons have dealt with HIV- and AIDS-infected inmates by isolating them from the rest of the prison population. Deprived of work, recreation, socialization, and rehabilitation, these inmates have dubbed the HIV/AIDS units the new death rows. Other prisons have left these ill inmates in the general prison population and instituted AIDS educational programs to enlist the ac-

ceptance and cooperation of the other prisoners and correctional officers. But this decision has sometimes backfired on officials, as HIV- and AIDS-infected inmates struck back at the system by trying to infect guards with the disease. Correctional officers have been bitten, spit on, spattered with infected blood, and served coffee laced with infected blood.

Managing problems

Some states, including California and New York, introduced what they call compassionate release parole to deal with the problem. That means that AIDS patients are released early so that they may die at home. This is not only a humane program, but it saves the prisons a great deal of money. Housing an AIDS patient costs a prison approximately forty thousand dollars more a year than housing a healthy inmate.

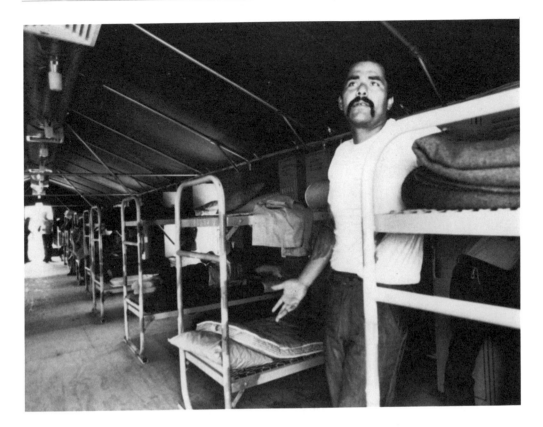

Whether it is true or not, the general feeling seems to be that AIDS, violence, gangs, drugs, and the other problems in prisons will become manageable if the problem of overcrowding is solved. Some people think the rate of crowding is decreasing. They point to California as an example. Although the number of prisoners there is still growing, the rate of increase has dropped off. In 1989 and 1990, for instance, California's prison population grew by over ten thousand people a year. In 1991 it grew by only six thousand.

This trend is not due to a decrease in crime: it appears to be the result of a letup in the war against drugs. And that letup is due to a change in police priorities caused by limited local budgets. In San Francisco, for example, 127 officers assigned to drug crimes made fifteen thousand ar-

A San Quentin inmate stands in a newly erected tent used to house inmates and ease overcrowding in the California prison. Without the protection of cells, some inmates in the tents fear violence from other inmates.

rests in 1987. By 1990 the drug unit had been reduced to 50 officers, and they made only eight hundred arrests.

If this trend continues nationwide, penologists may have the chance to prove their theory that overcrowding is what makes the other problems in prisons unmanageable. Based on the history of prisons, however, their chances do not look good. Prisons have historically been violent, disease-ridden places, even when overcrowding was less severe. And one of the few American prisons that is not overcrowded has had to use extraordinary means to bring its problems under control. That prison is the maximum-security federal penitentiary at Marion, Illinois.

Lockdown at Marion

The approximately 365 men imprisoned at Marion are deemed the nation's most dangerous and unmanageable prisoners. Most of them have come there from other prisons because they are gang leaders, escape artists, or incorrigible, violent troublemakers. And many of them are in prison for life. There is no overcrowding, because the number of inmates is limited by the number of cells. Each inmate must have an individual cell.

There are no rehabilitation programs at Marion. There is no communal dining, no work, no group recreation, no contact visits, and no classes. The prison is as harsh and punishing as the law and public opinion will allow. Almost all the inmates are locked into their cells in solitary confinement for twenty-three hours a day. According to *U.S. News & World Report*, Marion's philosophy is

> to psychologically emasculate a man, strip down his ego, crush his macho insolence and force him to conform to the strictest rules ever implemented in modern American penology. Only after he be-

haves under these conditions for a minimum of two years is he allowed to return to a regular maximum-security prison.

Marion was a normal maximum-security prison until 1983. But between 1980 and 1983 there were fourteen escape attempts, ten group disturbances, fifty-eight assaults on other inmates, and thirty-three attacks on correctional officers. Nine inmates and two guards were murdered. In October 1983 Marion was locked down (as this restrictive type of management is called) and has remained that way ever since. Now it is clean, quiet, and relatively safe. For some of the inmates this is a relief. "I used to be a predator in Atlanta [Federal Penitentiary]," said Marion inmate Richard Thompson. "Here, the atmosphere of violence is absent."

Right or wrong?

Prison reformers and prisoner rights activists say that Marion is the wrong way to solve prison problems; they think lockdown is cruel and unusual punishment. Although history indicates that idleness and isolation harm rather than help prisoners, Marion is evidence that lockdown can, at least, control crime and violence within prison walls.

Nevertheless, Marion will probably always be an exception. Except in emergencies, such as riots, few penologists are willing to turn prisons into institutions based solely on punishment. Penologists all agree, however, that the problems in today's prisons—overcrowding, violence, racial tension, and drug use, among others—must be solved before prisons can begin to achieve society's goals for them.

A guard patrols an older wing of the prison at Marion, Illinois, where a lockdown has helped reduce violence among inmates.

4

Alternative Sentencing

OF ALL THE PROBLEMS facing prisons, overcrowding has probably received the most attention in recent years. This may be because it is so obvious a symptom that something is wrong. Experts disagree over whether this issue deserves the prominence it has received. However, many contend that deeper problems will not be solved until overcrowded conditions have been relieved.

The most obvious solution to overcrowding is to send fewer offenders to prison. Yet simple solutions rarely are as simple as they first appear. This one is no exception. While most Americans can sympathize with the problems presented by overcrowding, they have no desire to see convicted offenders walking the streets of their communities—unpunished.

Creative solutions

The criminal justice system has had to seek ways of keeping offenders out of prison that will also satisfy the public's demand for punishment. The answer for the 1980s and 1990s is called alternative, or creative, sentencing.

The officials who deal most directly with this solution are the criminal court judges, because

(Opposite page) New arrivals at the Sumter County, Florida, Correctional Institution "Boot Camp" program march to the barracks. The caps hanging over the gate belonged to inmates who failed the program and were ordered to complete their sentences in prison.

they are the ones who sentence convicted criminals. When criminals are convicted of offenses that carry a mandatory sentence, they must be sent to prison, no matter how concerned the judges may be about prison conditions. In other cases judges can use their discretion in deciding how to punish the offenders who appear before them.

Trying public humiliation

Since the mid-1980s many judges have used their discretion to substitute alternative sentences for imprisonment. One example is Superior Court Judge Howard Broadman, who works in Visalia, a central California town of eighty thousand. He convicted thirty-year-old Russell Hackler, who had already been in prison once for robbery, of stealing two six-packs of beer from a supermarket. Because Hackler was a repeat offender, this conviction would normally have earned him four years in prison. Judge Broadman felt that prison would probably just criminalize him further. "If prison isn't going to work," the judge said, "maybe public humiliation will." So the judge designed and personally paid for a T-shirt that said MY RECORD AND TWO SIX PACKS EQUAL FOUR YEARS on the front and I AM ON FELONY PROBATION FOR THEFT on the back. Hackler was ordered to wear it for a year whenever he left his house.

A sentence of this type accomplishes several things. It helps decrease prison overcrowding. It also saves the taxpayers money. The average national cost of housing a prisoner for a year is $17,558. Most alternative sentencing arrangements cost much less than that, and some even require payment by the offender. In theory, alternative sentencing also satisfies the three goals of imprisonment. Judge Broadman intended for Hackler's public display of the T-shirt to both keep Hackler from further criminal activity and deter other people from robbery. He also hoped that reprieve from prison would help rehabilitate Hackler by giving him a second chance.

Limits

Hackler's T-shirt is only one example of a wide variety of possible alternative sentences. The range of alternatives used by judges is limited by only a few factors. One factor is the crime; another is the criminal. Alternative sentences are used mainly for first-time offenders convicted of nonviolent crimes, such as passing bad checks, tax evasion, fraud, and other so-called white-collar crimes. Alternative sentences are usually not given to habitual criminals or those who commit violent crimes such as rape, murder, and assault.

The types of programs available in a community can also influence alternative sentencing decisions. Say, for instance, that a judge wants to

Rather than going to prison, seventeen-year-old John McCrea was sentenced to a drug rehabilitation center. There, he received help with overcoming his drug habit.

sentence a drug offender to a residential drug rehabilitation program. Community residential programs and other alternatives not only relieve the crowding in prisons and cost less to operate, but they also do not criminalize first-time and nonviolent offenders the way prisons do. The theory is that if offenders are not criminalized by prison, they will be less apt to become repeat offenders. But if the community has no residential programs or if the programs are full, the judge cannot use that alternative.

Alternatives are also limited by the criminals' civil rights. Many judges have been accused of violating offenders' rights, and sometimes their sentences are overturned by a higher court. When Darlene Johnson appeared before Judge Broadman and pleaded guilty to brutally beating her children, the judge could have sent her to state

prison for four years. Instead he offered her the choice between prison and using Norplant, a form of birth control that is implanted in the arm, to prevent her from having any more children. Although Johnson agreed to use Norplant at first, later she appealed the sentence on the grounds that Judge Broadman had violated her reproductive rights.

To a *Time* magazine reporter, when Judge Broadman was asked how he would respond to statements that he violated Johnson's rights, he replied: "I say they're right. That's what courts do. Courts balance one right against another. And I was balancing her rights against the rights of her children."

A California doctor sentenced to live in the slum tenement he owned and refused to clean up wore this monitoring device around his ankle. The device signals a computer if the wearer leaves the premises.

Although Judge Broadman's sentences are perhaps the best known examples of judicial creativity in sentencing, he is by no means the only judge who devises alternative sentences. One sentenced a Los Angeles brain surgeon to spend thirty days in one of the roach- and rat-infested slum apartments he owned because he repeatedly failed to correct health and building code violations. Another judge sentenced a Texas hairdresser convicted of destroying a neighbor's property to give free haircuts to disabled children. In Oregon a demolition contractor convicted of theft was ordered to advertise his crime by buying space in two newspapers to publish his photograph and a public apology.

Probation

Many creative sentences involve a combination of punishments. Darlene Johnson, for example, was not only ordered to use Norplant, but she was also sentenced to a year in county jail and attending parenting classes and mental health counseling. Russell Hackler was on probation for the year he had to wear his T-shirt. Probationers, of-

A probation officer meets with a convict sentenced to probation. Probation has helped ease prison overcrowding, but burgeoning caseloads have overwhelmed understaffed probation offices.

fenders on probation, continue to live and work in the community, but they are supervised by a probation officer who oversees their behavior.

Probation has become the most common response to prison overcrowding. Although probationers are free to lead their own lives, they are under orders to obey certain rules, such as reporting to their probation officers regularly and not socializing with known criminals. Unfortunately, it seldom works that way. Because over 60 percent of the more than four million Americans under the custody of the criminal justice system are on probation, each probation officer usually supervises two hundred or more offenders. In some cities, such as Los Angeles, a probation officer's caseload can reach as high as one thousand probationers, creating an impossible task. Probation officers rarely have time to see the offenders in their charge face to face and have little or no control over their activities. The result is that probation as an alternative does not work for the majority of probationers. One study of 1,672 probationers found that 65 percent of them got into further trouble. Of those, 51 percent were arrested for new crimes, including murder, rape, and robbery, and the remainder violated the conditions of their probation.

Probation's failure to control crime and prevent recidivism is evident in Hackler's case: he burglarized a home while still wearing his T-shirt and ended up in prison again.

Intensive probation

While no alternative is a total success, several have demonstrated they can do a better job than probation in reducing recidivism and a better, and less expensive, job of deterring crime than can prisons. The most promising creative sentence, according to many experts, is intensive probation. Intensive probation differs from regular probation in several ways. In Georgia, for example, where this alternative started in 1982, probation officers supervise only about twenty-five offenders each. These offenders must meet face to face with their probation officers five times a week. They must conform to a mandatory curfew, be employed, perform 132 hours of community service, and pay a monthly fee for their supervision based on their ability to pay. They are subject to unannounced alcohol and drug testing and weekly checks to make sure they have not been arrested for any crimes.

A report by former Wisconsin corrections chief Walter J. Dickey on Wisconsin's intensive probation program describes how intensely Ed Ross, a probation officer in Grant, Wisconsin, handled the offenders he supervised. Besides involving the offender's family, the local community, and the state correctional department, Ross has frequent direct contacts with clients [probationers], particularly at the beginning of the supervisory relationship. . . . Over time, it does become clear that one result of the frequency and nature of the contacts is that they reflect and communicate to the clients a true concern about their welfare. . . . [Never] did a client leave a meeting with the vague understanding that he would look for a job. Rather, the client knew where he was to look, when, and that the agent would be back in touch on an appointed day for a report on how things went. . . . The client knew why whatever was being required was important.

Intensive probation programs in other states have also received praise. Records indicate that they are having an effect. Cal Thomas wrote in the *Washington Times* in 1990:

> Only 16 percent of all participants in [Georgia's intensive probation] program are rearrested within 18 months of completing the program. . . . In New Jersey, only 8 percent of [probationers] are rearrested for new crimes. In Illinois, the rate of rearrests for new crimes is only 5 percent.

House arrest

Another alternative sentence that has achieved considerable success is house arrest, a program in which offenders are imprisoned in their own homes. In some cases the offender must stay home at all times, except for attending church, therapy, and other officially sanctioned appointments. In other cases the offender is allowed to go to work during the day. House arrest is usually ordered in conjunction with probation.

To make sure they stay home, offenders on house arrest are monitored by electronic devices. The first monitoring device was introduced in 1985 and is still being used. It is an electronic ankle bracelet that sets off an alarm if offenders get more than about 150 feet from their telephones. Less expensive forms of electronic monitoring

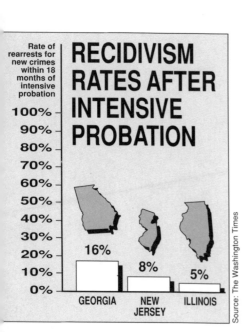

Rate of rearrests for new crimes within 18 months of intensive probation

RECIDIVISM RATES AFTER INTENSIVE PROBATION

100%
90%
80%
70%
60%
50%
40%
30%
20% — 16%
10% — 8% 5%
0%

GEORGIA NEW JERSEY ILLINOIS

Source: The Washington Times

Convicts sentenced to house arrest often wear a monitoring device around one ankle. The device immediately alerts law enforcement officials if the convict leaves the house.

through computerized telephones have since been introduced. In one system the computer records the sound of the offender's voice saying the names of twenty-two states. The computer calls the offender at random hours to ask for a different combination of eight state names, and if the wrong voice answers the question, the offender's probation officer is notified.

An even more sophisticated device, a video telephone, or videophone, not only shows offenders in their living rooms, but can also check blood-alcohol levels with a hand-held monitoring device called a Breathalyzer. Offenders, although they may feel uncomfortable that the government is watching their every move, usually prefer electronic monitoring to prison. The story of one appreciative offender appeared in *People* magazine. Maria Arnford, a Texas homemaker, was convicted of drug possession and drunk driving. She was sentenced to house arrest, where she was monitored by a videophone. Whenever this special telephone rang, she had to punch a button that sent her image back to Program Monitor, Inc., a private firm that owns and operates the equipment. If she did not punch the button, her probation officer would be notified. "This is the first [drug-free] time I can remember," said Arnford, whose behavior demonstrates that she is finally developing some self-discipline. "This program has been like a parent to me, the parent I never had."

Repaying the community

Another potentially effective creative sentence is community service, such as picking up trash, repairing homes in the slums, or volunteering in a hospital. In one unusual case a doctor convicted of selling drugs was ordered to practice medicine for seven years in Tombstone, Arizona, a town that had no doctor.

Community service is often used in conjunction with other programs, such as probation and house arrest. The theory behind community service as a punishment is that the public humiliation associated with it will act as a deterrent to future crime. Furthermore, it forces the offender to accept the responsibility of paying society back for violating its laws. Studies have found recidivism rates for community service programs to be as low as 3 percent.

Victim restitution, compensating the victim for most or all of the financial loss caused by the offense, has also gained popularity as a creative sentence. For instance, an offender who vandalizes someone's property is ordered to pay for repair of the property. An offender who injures someone is ordered to pay the medical expenses. Not only are the victims somewhat compensated for their losses, but, say Charles Colson and Daniel Van Ness in their book, *Convicted*: "Offenders benefit from assuming personal responsibility and performing purposeful work as well. Paying back someone they have wronged allows a criminal to understand and deal with the consequences of his actions." In theory this can lead to rehabilitation by changing the way offenders think and behave. It is particularly effective when the offender must meet with the victim face to face to discuss the restitution and apologize.

Boot camp

The most extreme alternative to prison is boot camp, which was initiated in Georgia in 1983 for male offenders under the age of twenty-five. Boot camp is often referred to as "shock incarceration." Based on the basic training concepts of military boot camp, these camps are designed to scare young offenders away from crime and whatever mistaken notions they harbor about an easy life in prison. At the boot camp in Forsyth, Georgia, the program begins with the sergeant's greeting: "You have just walked into the worst nightmare you ever dreamed. I don't like you. I have no use for you, Maggot . . . and it matters not one damn to me whether you make it here or get tossed into prison."

The offenders' heads are shaved, their cigarettes are taken away, their personal possessions are locked up, and they are given blue-and-white-striped uniforms. The physical regimen is grueling. For ninety days they rise at 5:00 A.M. No one speaks without permission. Inmates clean their barracks twice daily and are expected to perform hard labor without complaint. Rules are strictly enforced and all infractions are punished.

"Being scared is the point," Sgt. Tommy Williamson of the Forsyth camp told *Life* magazine. "We break them down as hard and fast as we can, push them as hard as they can be pushed before they blow. Then we can start building them up, giving them some self-discipline."

Added the camp's first warden, Truett Goodwin:

Tears flow as the harsh psychological treatment of the boot camp alternative to prison breaks down this inmate's defenses.

Our job is to provide them with an experience that can help them on the outside. They're not going to leave here any smarter, but we can provide some structure and discipline that they obviously have never gotten. We can't fix the . . . problems that led to crime in the first place, but we can influence what they do next.

Some of the boot camp graduates are enthusiastic about the program. "When I came through the front door, I had to become a man in about 30 seconds," said one nineteen-year-old probation violator. "I wish I had come here the first time I got in trouble." Another twenty-two-year-old boot camp graduate has since completed his high school equivalency and entered college. "It's ninety days of talking to yourself," he said, "and looking at yourself and getting a picture of the direction you were heading. Now I want to get on with my life."

Many boot camp graduates do get on with their lives. With only a 20 percent recidivism rate in

Prison boot camp instructors show new arrivals the correct way to line up as they are marched off to the barber to have their heads shaved.

the first three years, the Georgia program convinced other states to initiate similar programs. In 1990, 11,226 offenders were sent to boot camps around the country.

Equal justice?

As promising as all these alternatives seem, several issues have been raised concerning their use. One major issue involves judicial discretion, which is the amount of freedom judges have to make sentencing decisions. Judges on the state level have a certain amount of discretion in sentencing. This means that offenders who commit the same crime in the same state, or even in the same city, may receive totally different punishments. For example, while Russell Hackler was being sentenced to his T-shirt and a year's probation, other repeat robbers in California were being sentenced to four years in prison. Many critics think such discrepancies violate the American principle of equal justice for all. They argue that four years in prison is a much harsher punishment than the one Hackler received.

These critics want judicial discretion on the state level to be limited by sentencing guidelines, as it is on the federal level. Federal judicial discretion is limited by general guidelines that specify a range of sentencing options for each particular offense. When sentencing someone convicted of, for example, income tax evasion, a federal judge must choose a sentence from among those approved for that offense. Since the sentencing options are all considered appropriate punishments for the offense, there is more assurance that equal justice will be served.

Another complaint voiced against alternative sentencing is that it perpetuates class and racial bias. Well-to-do offenders, critics say, get alternative sentences that place them in community ser-

Although they comprise a relatively small percentage of the general population, blacks, together with Latinos, make up a large part of the U.S. prison population.

vice programs, and poor offenders go to prison. What is more, these critics say, white criminals receive alternative sentences more often than do blacks, Latinos, and other minorities.

Statistics confirm that most prison inmates are poor. Statistics also show that prisons actually house more whites than blacks, Latinos, or other minorities. But proportionately, or relative to their numbers in the general population, blacks and Latinos are overrepresented in prisons. For example, one of every five black men serves time in prison while only one of every thirty-seven white men serves a prison sentence.

It is difficult to know for certain whether these numbers are a result of class and racial biases by sentencing judges and juries or a combination of many factors that may include bias. The nature of the crime, for example, is an important factor in alternative sentencing. Those who commit violent crimes are rarely given the chance to serve an alternative sentence. Yet even when comparable crimes are at issue, sentences vary. Sometimes these sentences seem to bear out complaints of inequity.

John Zaccaro Jr., son of former vice presidential candidate Geraldine Ferraro, was convicted of selling cocaine in 1988. He served a total of four months of house arrest in a Vermont $1,500-a-month, two-bedroom apartment with weekly maid service. On the other hand, remarked a Michigan corrections official quoted in John DiIulio's book, *No Escape*, "I've seen poor black kids rot in crowded jails for selling less. . . ."

"Custom-tailored sentences"

A third major criticism of alternative sentences is that they do not accomplish their primary goal, that of relieving prison overcrowding. Critics say there is some evidence that many offenders who receive alternative sentences are the type of offenders who would never have gone to prison in any case. They would simply have been put on probation. Therefore, critics say, alternative sentences are not addressing overcrowding problems.

Despite these issues, few people advocate the elimination of creative sentencing. Managed properly, not only can it help relieve crowding in prisons, but it can also provide success in many areas where prisons fail. Wrote James Bennet in the *Washington Monthly*:

> We've tried [being] soft on crime, and that didn't work. Now we've tried [being] tough on crime, and the results have been just as unimpressive. Maybe we should try [being] smart on crime. As state and federal lock-ups approach gridlock, the challenge . . . is to take the elegant, custom-tailored sentence and start marketing it retail.

5

Changing Prisons from the Inside Out

CREATIVE SENTENCING keeps some people out of prison, but it alone cannot solve the problems of prisons. Prison managers and makers of public policy know that they must look beyond alternative sentences for answers, and they have done that. Over the past two decades their search has been hastened by judicial intervention, that is, rulings made by judges about unacceptable prison conditions and practices.

Court orders

Judicial intervention in prison management began in 1969 with the U.S. Supreme Court ruling in the case of *Johnson v. Avery*. In that case an Arkansas prison inmate challenged the policy that allowed floggings with a leather strap. The Supreme Court ruled that this practice was unconstitutional because it violated the inmate's right not to be subjected to cruel and unusual punishment. Aside from deciding the case itself, this ruling opened the way for further judicial intervention in prison practices. By the early 1970s judges were beginning to hear more and more

(Opposite page) Inmates play basketball in an outdoor court on prison grounds. Improved recreational opportunities are one response to concerns about poor prison conditions.

71

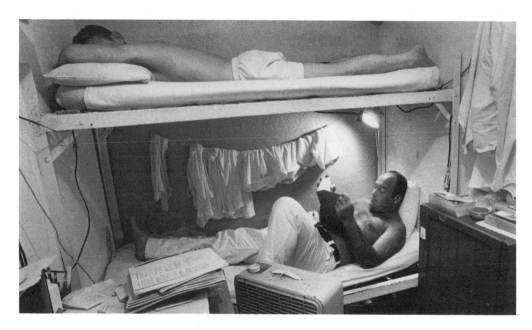

Two inmates share a cell measuring nine by six feet. In 1981 the U.S. Supreme Court refused to hold that double-bunking in prison cells was cruel and unusual punishment.

cases alleging dehumanizing conditions inside the nation's prisons. They intervened on such issues as food services, sanitation, health care, and especially overcrowding.

By 1992 over forty states were under court order to reduce overcrowding. Many people felt the courts had gone too far with their orders and had succeeded only in making prison management more difficult. "Though the Supreme Court in 1981 refused to hold that double-bunking in prison cells violates the Constitution," wrote Eugene H. Methvin in the *National Review*, "lower judges still declare unconstitutional cells that may be as large as eighty square feet—more than twice the size of nuclear submarine officers' quarters accommodating two or three men."

But many people agreed with a 1988 federal circuit court decision that stated: "Judges are not wardens, but we must act as wardens to the limited extent that unconstitutional prison conditions force us to intervene when those responsible for the conditions have failed to act."

Under court order to reduce the crowding in their facilities, prison managers had only one option. Since they had no control over the number of prisoners sent to their prisons, they had to accelerate the flow of prisoners released from their prisons. To do this, at least thirteen states began emergency release programs.

Early release

Under these programs, when the state prison population reaches a given maximum and stays at that figure for, usually, a month, a designated percentage of the prisoners must be released. Michigan, for example, handles this by moving all parole dates up by ninety days. (Parole today is essentially the same as probation, except that a parolee has served time in prison and a probationer has not.) Those inmates who become eligible for parole because of this ninety-day gift are

CRIME AND PUNISHMENT

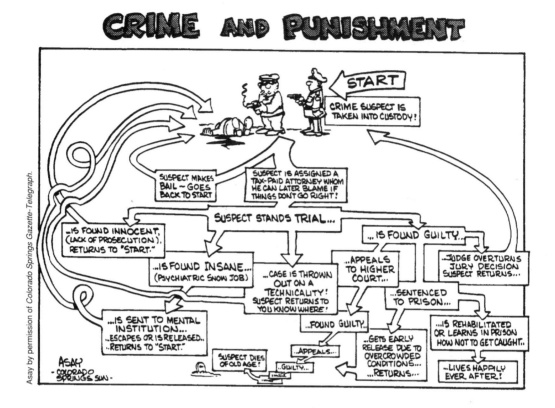

released. This system of release continues until the prison population is reduced to 95 percent of the prison's capacity.

Some states have instituted broad early-release programs whereby almost all prisoners are released early on parole as a matter of course. In fact, although there are some inmates who will never be released, most convicted criminals do not serve even half their sentences behind bars. Even murderers, rapists, and robbers spend about 50 percent of their sentences on parole in the community. Very often these violent offenders have been paroled to make room in prison for low-level drug offenders.

According to M. Kay Harris of Temple University, these release programs "have had more significant impact on prison crowding than strate-

gies for directing offenders to alternative programs." But, Harris adds, "Expediting release of
prisoners while doing nothing to stem the flow is
like bailing water from a boat without repairing
the gaping hole."

The revolving door

Early release is a temporary solution to overcrowding not only because it does not stop the
flow of offenders into prison, but also because
many of the offenders released early commit
more crimes and end up back in prison. In
Florida, for example, Michael Patrick Wilson
went to prison for burglary at the age of eighteen.
At age twenty he went to prison for burglary
again. At age twenty-one he went to prison for
kidnapping and rape; at age twenty-six, for attempted burglary. Each time he was released
early, the last time after serving less than eighteen
months. A month after he was released the fourth
time, he murdered a seventy-three-year-old
preacher who caught him in the act of burglariz-
ing his church.

The news is full of such stories. A burglar released early committed five hundred burglaries in
seven months. A rapist, sentenced to a minimum
of ten years, was released in six years and raped
and killed a woman. A paroled killer broke into
two homes and killed three people. A study of
twenty-one thousand prisoners released early in
Illinois in the 1980s revealed some amazing statistics. After their release an unspecified number of
those prisoners were responsible for 23 homicides,
32 rapes, 262 arsons, 681 robberies, 2,472 burglaries, 2,571 assaults, and more than 8,000 other
crimes, at a cost of $304 million to the victims.

Because of these and similar cases, many penologists and members of the public want early
release stopped. Even judicial intervention has

William Barr, U.S. attorney general in the Bush administration, believes the answer to prison overcrowding is not to release prisoners but to build more prisons.

been eased. In January 1992 in *Rufo v. Inmates of Suffolk County Jail*, the U.S. Supreme Court issued a ruling that makes it easier for states to challenge court-imposed limits on prison populations. Now states can challenge court limits when the solution to overcrowding causes more problems than it solves.

A clear choice?

Also in 1992, U.S. attorney general William Barr announced that federal lawyers would help the states challenge those limits. Said Barr:

> The only way to reduce violent crime is to incarcerate these chronic violent offenders, give them long prison sentences and keep them locked up in prison until they have served their full sentence. The choice is clear: more prison space or more crime.

Many people agree with Barr. Building more prisons seems like one way to deal with prison overcrowding. In fact, in mid-1992 the United States was building or planned to build prison space for 169,921 more prisoners. Cost is the main reason why the nation is not building prisons even faster. It is often difficult to persuade the public to support expenditures for new prisons.

Many members of the general public do not consider overcrowding a problem: they believe that criminals deserve whatever they get. Also, public funds are now needed for many other pressing social problems, and the cost of prison construction is high. Prison construction costs are measured in terms of cost per bed. This amount refers to the portion of building and equipment costs for housing one inmate. The average cost per prison bed is now almost $48,000, and the cost has occasionally run as high as $150,000.

By neglecting prison construction because of cost, however, the public may be making a mistake. In 1987 economist Edwin Zedlewski did a study for the National Institute of Justice to analyze how cost-effective prisons are. He estimated that housing each prisoner for a year costs $25,000. Using crime statistics, he also estimated that the typical offender commits 187 crimes a year at a cost of $2,300 per crime in property losses, physical injury, and suffering. Thus the typical offender at large in the community costs society 187 times $2,300, or $430,100 a year. Zedlewski found that spending $25,000 a year to imprison a typical offender actually saves the public $405,100 every year that the offender is behind bars.

The difficulty, many penologists say, is that we can never build enough prisons. No matter how many are built, they just keep filling up. As Joan Muller, former director of a study entitled "American Prisons and Jails," wrote: "Many have cautioned that more prisons may simply buy more prisoners and the same crowded conditions

Chuck Asay, by permission of the Colorado Springs Gazette-Telegraph.

Construction on a new prison begins. The concrete modular units being lowered into place are ready-made, or prefabricated. Their use helps keep construction costs down.

as before."

This view has never been proved or disproved. Although there is some historical evidence that prisons do rapidly become crowded as fast as they are built, it may just be that officials have always failed to plan ahead properly and have built too few prisons. With construction costs rising constantly, the chances are this argument will never be resolved.

"Sell the walls"

Some penologists, however, think they have the answer to prison overcrowding and escalating costs. With few exceptions American prisons have traditionally been built and operated by the state and federal governments. These penologists want to change this. They want to "sell the walls," that is, turn prison construction and operation over to private industry. High recidivism rates and rising crime, they say, prove that government cannot make prisons work. They feel that private corrections firms can do a better job for less money and still make a profit. In the 1980s a number of private firms, including Corrections Corporation of America, U.S. Corrections Corporation, and Wackenhut, began building and running prisons to take advantage of this trend.

Privatization, as this is called, is not a new idea. In fact, in the nineteenth and early twentieth centuries it was quite common. Texas, for example, leased its penitentiary to private contractors during the nineteenth century. "For a few dollars per month per convict," wrote John DiIulio in *No Escape,*

> the contractors were allowed to sublease their charges to farmers, tanners, and other businessmen. It was not long before the inmates began to appear in poor clothing and without shoes. Worked mercilessly, most convicts died within

seven years of their incarceration. Not surprisingly, escapes and escape attempts were frequent, and some inmates were driven to suicide. Others maimed themselves to get out of work or as a pathetic form of protest.

That earlier era of privatization ended amid scandals and public outcry from journalists, politicians, and prison managers, and many critics of the system have not forgotten. They say it is immoral to put prisoners in the hands of private companies who are in business to make a profit. To ensure they make a profit, critics argue, private companies may neglect the welfare of prisoners under their charge. And they may exert pressure on government policy to ensure that sentencing laws provide a steady supply of prisoners to fill their cells. Also, critics say, laws are made by the public, and only the public should have the right to punish those who break the laws.

Debate over privatization

Proponents of privatization say that is nonsense. As long as the sentence of imprisonment comes from the public courts and the prisons are supervised by the government, it should not matter whether day-to-day prison operations are run by public or private entities. They point out that under government regulation life in private prisons cannot be any worse than life in public prisons. Prisoners themselves have been known to prefer private prisons, where they sometimes receive such amenities as color televisions and heated food trays.

Moreover, say those in favor of privatization, since private companies have to invest a great deal of money to build, equip, and staff their prisons, they will do nothing to jeopardize their investment. As Charles R. Ring said in the *Wall Street Journal*:

> They [the private companies] will have to balance their desire to cut costs with their need for long-term contracts. Furthermore, many of the companies seeking private prison contracts want to operate facilities in several states. Such companies will not wish to jeopardize future contracts by running substandard institutions. Reputable private prison operators have a vested interest in promoting enforcement of government standards in order to deter fly-by-night outfits that could, by association, taint the entire industry.

The moral issues over privatization may never be solved, but one thing is clear: private prisons cost the government less money. When a private firm takes over the operation of an existing prison, there is a 10 percent saving. When a private firm operates a prison it designed and built itself, the saving is 15 percent. The difference is partly because private firms design prisons that require fewer employees, and payroll is 75 percent of the operating costs. Moreover, a private firm can build a prison at a 20 percent saving because it does not have to deal with costly government-purchasing regulations.

The concept catches on

These savings are what has made private corrections a growing business. It started with contracts for support services behind bars, such as food provision and medical care. It expanded to community correctional services and programs, such as drug rehabilitation, halfway houses, and work-release programs. From there it grew to include secure juvenile facilities and federal detention centers for illegal aliens. By the mid-1980s there were over twenty firms seeking contracts to operate the prisons themselves.

In 1985 Corrections Corporation of America (CCA), a leader in the field, made a bid to take over the entire Tennessee prison system. The bid failed, but CCA did get contracts for federal detention centers, halfway houses, and numerous county jails. In 1986 both California and Kentucky gave contracts for private care of state prisoners. U.S. Corrections Corporation was awarded a contract for a minimum-security state prison in Marion, Kentucky. In California, both Eclectic Communications, Inc., and Management and Training Corporation began operating facilities for parolees who were returned to custody for parole violations.

The concept began spreading. In 1987, for example, Texas awarded contracts for four private state prisons. By mid-1992 private firms were responsible for about twenty thousand prison beds, with another five thousand under construction. That is still only a small proportion of all prison beds, but private firms are using them to try to prove that not only can they operate prisons cheaper, but that they can do it better. As a *Chattanooga* [Tennessee] *Times* newspaper editorial said: "Private enterprise should be given a chance to find the corrections solutions that have eluded the public sector."

Some experts believe privatization has that potential, particularly since private management has always had a better reputation for efficiency, motivation, and innovation than public management. For instance, W. James Ellison wrote in the *Cumberland Law Review*:

> Privatization of corrections has the potential to expose the public penal sector to the vitality and flexibility of private enterprise—to private sector management efficiencies and principles of competitive business; to methodologies designed to meet and respond to ever-changing penological circumstances; to experimentation with new modes of corrections, uninhibited by the bureaucracies and politics inherent in the management and operation of public penal facilities.

Prison inmates learn to use computers. Some experts believe that privately owned and operated prisons can provide better facilities and programs for prisoners than can publicly run prisons.

For now, however, it is still too early to tell if this potential can be realized.

Concerns

In the meantime many penologists believe that privatization will never be accepted on a large scale. One reason for this is the uneasiness some people feel about private companies performing public tasks. Edward Sagarin and Jess Maghan discussed this concern in the *Angolite*, a magazine published by prisoners at the Louisiana State Penitentiary:

> Racial and ethnic minorities and low social-class whites are disproportionately represented in the American prison population. Today they are under the care and control of a government in which blacks, Hispanics and others are gaining a small share of power, at least a foothold. Corporate America is upper-class white. Only a few of its hirelings are minority people. Privatization places in the hands of the haves a tool to exploit and further enrich themselves at the expense of the have nots.

Privatization proponents also worry about resistance from those currently working in the penal field. Rather than giving up the field to private managers, these penologists say, the skills of public managers should be upgraded. This will keep prisons in the public sector, where many people believe they belong, and help public managers solve many of the problems plaguing prisons.

Some prison managers may balk at the notion that management style is a key factor in solving problems behind bars. But there is evidence that better prison management is the answer to some problems. This evidence can be seen in cases where overcrowded prisons full of violent offenders are run with a minimum of problems. In every case the relative smoothness of the operations can be traced back to sound management.

John DiIulio cites the case of the California

Men's Colony (CMC), a maximum-security prison in San Luis Obispo. In the mid-1980s CMC was operating at about 120 percent of its capacity. Almost all of the more than two thousand inmates were repeat offenders, and 25 percent of them were classified as dangerous enough to belong in one of California's two highest security prisons, San Quentin and Folsom (which were too overcrowded to accept them). By 1989 the inmate population at CMC had reached sixty-five hundred to seven thousand, making it one of the most heavily populated prisons in a capitalist country. The percentage of hard-core and hard-to-handle prisoners had also increased.

Yet, through all those years, CMC had remained, according to DiIulio, the safest, cleanest, most program-oriented, most cost-effective maximum-security prison in California, and one of the best such prisons in the nation. Rates of inmate-on-inmate assaults remained low, as did rates of inmate assaults on staff; in fact, rates of violence actually *decreased* as the prison became more crowded. Meanwhile, cellblocks continued to sparkle and prison industry programs hummed. Inmate participation in all sorts of educational and vocational programs grew, recreational facilities were expanded and improved, and the already far above average institutional meals were diversified and enriched. All these improvements were achieved while CMC had the highest inmate-to-staff ratios and the lowest annual per inmate expenditures of any maximum-security prison in California.

"But how?" asks DiIulio. The answer, he says, lies in the management style of the prison's former warden, Wayne Estelle. First, Estelle believed in a management style called Management by Walking Around. "He has been fond of walking *and* talking around the prison, seeing for himself what staff and inmates are doing, asking questions, and answering them," says DiIulio. Second, Estelle stressed results. He focused on whether the prison was clean, the violence rate low, the escape rate zero, the classes orderly. He did not focus on how those results were achieved. Reports DiIulio:

> His three basic rules are—"no dirt, no graffiti, no bad behavior." His staff knows that . . . [making excuses for not producing results] does not win his heart, and that he does not like to deal with the same inmate problem (or see the same cigarette butt on the industry plant floor) twice.

Third, the staff knew that "as much as he values inmate participation in work programs and educational activities, security and control come first." The top priority was to protect the inmates in their charge and keep them from escaping. Fourth, Estelle rarely made innovations, but when

Wayne Estelle believed in talking often with prison inmates and staff.

he did, he did it slowly and informed inmates and staff of the reasons well in advance so they had time to adjust.

Fifth, he "cultivated positive relations with San Luis Obispo [County] officials, offering the services of inmate volunteers to assist in certain forestry and fire-fighting activities." This gave Estelle ties to influential people in the community who could affect prison funding, laws regarding prisons, and public opinion. Finally, while prison managers stayed an average of only three years on the job, Estelle was at CMC for most of his career. That gave him the time to understand the prison, make influential alliances in the community, and institute needed changes.

Deeper issues

If the management style used by Estelle and others like him can save our troubled prisons, the answer seems to lie in teaching this style to all prison managers. Unfortunately, it is not that simple. Even if it is not true, as many people say, that good managers are born, not made, managers' personalities have a great deal to do with whether or not a particular style works for them. Attitudes can be instilled and skills and techniques taught, but personalities cannot be changed by others.

Good management, alternative sentencing, more prisons, and privatization can all contribute to the solution of problems in prison. But the real issue goes deeper than that. The real issue is whether or not prisons really can deter and control crime and rehabilitate criminals. Penologists have been tossing this question around for two hundred years without any conclusive results. It is time for them to concentrate on a realistic appraisal of what prisons actually can achieve and how best to go about achieving it.

Inmate volunteers from CMC assist with firefighting efforts.

6

Setting Realistic Goals

PRISONS IN THE United States have historically demonstrated that all they can do well is punish, yet Americans still want their prisons to deter and control crime and rehabilitate criminals. Experts have mixed opinions about whether or not it is even reasonable to expect prisons to accomplish these goals.

Many experts agree with the National Advisory Commission on Criminal Justice Standards and Goals, which issued a report that said:

> The failure of major institutions to reduce crime is incontestable. . . . Institutions do succeed in punishing, but they do not deter. . . . They change the committed offender, but the change is more likely to be negative than positive. It is no surprise that institutions have not been more successful in reducing crime. The mystery is that they have not contributed even more to increasing crime.

Other experts feel that prisons can accomplish their goals. They agree with the summary of Patrick A. Langan's study entitled "America's Soaring Prison Population," which appeared in *Science* magazine. The summary states that annual surveys have shown that rising incarceration rates have been accompanied by gradual reductions in U.S. crime rates since 1973. "The possi-

(Opposite page) A youth languishes in a holding cell. Imprisonment has proved to be an effective punishment, but its ability to rehabilitate is less certain.

bility that rising incarceration rates are helping to reduce crime must be weighed in debates about America's prisons."

Langan is just one of a number of researchers who have conducted studies to find out what prisons can and cannot do. These researchers think penologists can make prisons work if they maintain realistic expectations and heed the research results. In his book *Confronting Crime*, Elliott Currie does a good job of summarizing those results.

Punishment as deterrent

There are actually two kinds of deterrence. One is individual deterrence, that is, the hope that punishing criminals by sending them to prison will keep those criminals from committing more crimes after they are released. The second is general deterrence, the hope that the threat of punishment by imprisonment will keep people from committing crimes in the first place.

According to sociologist Charles Tittle, general deterrence is apparently "rooted almost entirely in how people perceive the potential for negative reactions from interpersonal acquaintances." In other words, most potential offenders fear prison only when it would earn them the disrespect of family and peers. Such disapproval might work in stable families and communities where good behavior is valued and rewarded. But it is not apt to work in those segments of society that have the highest crime rates. In gangs, for example, peers actually give the most respect to those members who have been to prison for violent crimes.

This attitude helps explain why the threat of prison has not been an effective general deterrent to crime. Short of the impossible goal of developing an ideal society in which every community is stable and rewards law-abiding behavior, little can be done about crime. But something can be done about another obstacle to effective general deterrence. Criminals know that the threat of punishment often is an empty one. Even in this get-tough-on-crime era, criminals have a very good chance of escaping punishment.

After two hundred years, the issue of whether prisons deter and control crime and rehabilitate offenders remains unsettled.

Empty threats

More than half the felonies committed in the United States are not reported to the police. Often this is because the victims know the offenders personally and are reluctant to see them arrested.

Of the crimes that are actually reported, only about 20 percent end in an arrest. This is because there are often not enough police officers to follow up on all crimes closely. Also, many times there are not enough clues to allow the police to find the offender, especially when no witnesses will speak up.

The chances are that once this small percentage of suspected felons has been arrested, they will be offered the chance to plea bargain. That is, they will be allowed to plead guilty to a lesser charge rather than take the chance of being convicted in court for a more serious crime. For instance, a suspected felon arrested for mugging (assault and robbery) might be offered a deal to plead guilty to assault only. That lesser charge might earn the mugger probation instead of three years in prison. Plea bargaining is commonly used to relieve the backlog in court cases and to save money, since holding a trial is expensive.

Because plea bargaining is so common, less than 30 percent of the already small percentage of suspected felons actually arrested will be charged with a felony and go to trial. Approximately 12 percent of those trials will end with an acquittal, a not-guilty verdict. Of those felons who are convicted, only about 60 percent will be sent to prison. The rest will receive alternative sentences. On the average, when all is said and done, less than 2 percent of all felony crimes result in imprisonment.

Does crime pay?

Given these figures, it is no wonder the threat of imprisonment is not deterring crime. For many criminals crime does pay. It does not take long for offenders to figure out that their chances of going to prison are very small.

Yet studies show that imprisonment is one way to deter crime, as long as prison is the assured consequence of committing crime. This can be done, but only through great effort and expense. The public would have to be convinced to report every crime. Many more police would have to be hired.

"Achieving such a goal," wrote David C. Anderson in *Crimes of Justice*,

> would require revolutionary upheaval in the court system as judges and prosecutors and defense attorneys altered ways of thinking and acting they

have followed for decades. And it would require immense public expenditures to build the prison space. For the sake of prison cells, legislators would have to approve unpopular tax increases or diversion of money from such fundamentals as public schools, public health, and mass transit.

The shock of going to prison may be the best crime deterrent that imprisonment offers.

So far Americans have not been willing to make these sacrifices to increase general deterrence.

The shock effect

Individual deterrence, however, would be much less costly to improve. The prevailing theory is that the more severe the punishment, that is, the longer the prison sentence, the more deterrence there will be. According to Elliott Currie, studies show just the opposite:

As far back as the end of the sixties, the National Commission on the Causes and Prevention of Violence reviewed the evidence on the relationship between sentence length and recidivism; had their conclusions been heeded, we might have been spared some of the human and social cost of the "prison boom" of the following decade. The commission found that longer sentences did not consistently reduce recidivism rates—and sometimes seemed to increase them.

This and other studies have come to the same conclusion: longer sentences not only do not deter ex-convicts from committing more crimes, but they actually appear to promote recidivism. This negative effect most likely comes from criminalization.

Other studies have shown that the most effective part of imprisonment, the part that provides the most deterrence, is the initial shock of incarceration. After three to six months the shock wears off, and the deterrence effect of imprisonment declines rapidly. What this suggests is that the way to increase the effectiveness of individual deterrence, that is, reduce recidivism, is not to impose long sentences as the courts have been doing, but to impose short, mandatory sentences. In that way, every offender would have to go through shock incarceration, as this short expo-

Short sentences may be more effective than long ones in deterring crime, but the public desires to keep criminals off the streets by imposing long prison terms..

"ARE YOU ENJOYING YOUR REHABILITATION?"

sure to prison has been called, but would not remain in prison long enough to become incorrigibly criminalized.

Short sentences

Although short, mandatory sentences would initially cause problems by increasing prison overcrowding, in the long run they would reduce it. With less recidivism, there would be fewer offenders returning to prison. Also, there would be an even faster turnover of prisoners, especially as inmates serving today's longer sentences gradually finish their terms. Of course, short sentences are not right for every offender. Violent, hardened criminals would still have to be kept in prison, some for life, to protect society.

Short, mandatory sentences for most offenders are a solution that can be put into effect now. The main obstacle is the public's desire to punish offenders severely and get them off the streets for a long time. The best answer to that attitude is public education. If the public really understood that longer sentences actually produced more crime, public opinion might change.

Incapacitation as crime control

Imprisonment always controls crime in society to some extent. While offenders are in prison, they cannot commit crime. However, the amount of crime controlled by imprisonment is quite small. There is a distressingly large number of serious crimes in the United States every day. Since less than 2 percent of them result in imprisonment, it is evident that many criminals are still on the streets. The police will never be able to catch all of them. The courts will never be able to convict all of them. The United States will never be able to afford to keep all of them in prison. Nor is prison the best punishment for every offender.

Studies have shown that a large proportion of crimes are committed by a relatively small number of repeat offenders, the so-called career or habitual criminals. Therefore, some penologists think the best answer to crime control may be what is called selective incapacitation. First-time felons would be screened, and those who fit the profile of career criminals would be given a long sentence. They would not have the opportunity to become repeat offenders—at least, not for a long time.

Being able to predict which offenders will become career criminals and nipping that career in the bud is a very appealing idea. It would mean that incapacitation was finally controlling crime. Sen. Edward Kennedy, a liberal reformer, has praised selective incapacitation as offering "the possibility of concentrating scarce and costly prison resources on those most likely to commit crimes."

Sen. Edward Kennedy, a liberal reformer, supports the idea of using selective incapacitation to control crime.

The difficulty with selective incapacitation lies in the screening process, that is, trying to identify potential habitual criminals. Peter Greenwood and his colleagues at the Rand Corporation, a public policy research organization, are largely responsible for developing the concept of selective incapacitation. According to Elliott Currie:

> The Rand researchers claim to have developed newer and better means to sort out potential high-rate offenders from the rest. Ideally, this should mean that we can achieve a better level of crime prevention by locking up those high-raters for longer periods, without greatly adding to the prison space we already have—since the same prediction techniques theoretically also allow us to pick out less troublesome offenders and sentence them to less stringent terms.

The Rand researchers studied twenty-two hundred inmates in Texas, Michigan, and California and came up with seven characteristics they say can predict future career robbers and burglars. Those seven characteristics are: incarceration for more than a year in the two-year period before arrest; a prior conviction for the type of crime being predicted; a juvenile conviction before the age of sixteen; commitment to a state or federal juvenile institution; heroin or barbiturate use in the two years before the current arrest; heroin or barbiturate use as a juvenile; and being employed less than half of the two-year period before the current arrest.

Some researchers believe they can predict whether this youthful offender and others like him will be career criminals.

Habitual criminals

The Rand study predicted the effect selective incapacitation would have on the criminal justice system:

> If the sentencing policy were changed to provide longer terms for the high-rate offenders and much shorter terms for the predicted low- and medium-rate offenders, we estimated that there would be

approximately ten percent fewer robberies in California by adults and a reduction in the prison population of approximately five percent. A ten percent reduction in robberies may sound like a small number. However, given a rate of 150,000 robberies per year, we're talking about 15,000 robberies. We are also talking about a five percent reduction in the number of people locked up for robbery, that's 500 or 600 people or the equivalent of a small prison.

The Rand characteristics are similar to those already being used to identify habitual criminals in today's courts. Usually habitual criminals are given longer prison sentences than lesser offenders. But those criminals have already become career criminals. In selective incapacitation the characteristics would be used to predict future criminal behavior. That is why selective incapacitation will not work, say the critics. They think it is impossible to predict future criminal behavior. Social scientist Marc Miller states that "our current ability to predict long-term violent behavior is no better than one accurate prediction out of every three."

Because of this low rate of accuracy, dangerous offenders might be missed and offenders who are not dangerous might receive longer prison sentences than they deserve. The latter group would pay the price for this policy with their freedom. Many people think that price is too high to pay, even though selective incapacitation would work for society in general. Therefore, this potentially effective policy has been put aside until more reliable methods of prediction are developed.

Rehabilitation

Regardless of the prevailing theory about rehabilitation, penologists have always wanted prisons to reform criminals in order to stop recidivism and turn the prisoners into productive, law-abiding citizens. They are encouraged by recent studies that show some rehabilitation programs can be successful sometimes with some people.

Research by Paul Gendreau, research director at Centracare Saint John Inc. in New Brunswick, Canada, and others has begun to pinpoint the types of programs that can succeed with offenders. Gendreau and his colleagues "do not claim that correctional rehabilitation is without problems or that it offers a panacea [cure-all] to the crime problem," but they do say that "a growing body of data suggests not only that many interventions are successful but also that it is becoming increasingly possible to decipher the principles of effective treatment."

The single most important element of successful rehabilitation programs is the way they are organized and managed. Programs cannot succeed

Careful screening of first-time offenders may determine the likelihood of their becoming career criminals. This information can be useful for deciding whether a longer prison term is worthwhile.

unless they are run by concerned, energetic, competent people. Successful programs also build respect for lawful authority and increase the offenders' problem-solving skills, including those related to accepting responsibility for their actions.

Effective treatment involves support from the community to encourage the positive responses offenders need from society. For instance, it provides positive personal relationships and role models for the offenders. Effective treatment also enlists the aid of as many community resources, both human and financial, as possible. Finally, few programs succeed unless they provide some type of continuing support for the participants after the program has ended.

Working with horses

The Vocational Horse Training Program initiated as a pilot project at the California Correctional Center at Susanville in 1987 is an interesting example of the type of program that can succeed. The U.S. Bureau of Land Management developed the program to enable inmates to train wild mustangs captured from federal land. Program participants train the horses to accept a bridle and saddle before they are sold to private buyers. In training the horse, the inmate learns self-confidence, patience, trust, self-discipline, and good work habits.

For more than one inmate, this goal has been achieved. For example, after Bob Miller graduated from the program, he was hired as a horse handler by a California rancher. "I'm confident I'm not going to come back [to prison]," he told *People* magazine, "because I've learned something that I enjoy." Miller learned patience because, "You have to wait until the horse decides to go. You can't carry him. I've got a temper, but I've learned to control it."

Inmates at California's Folsom State Prison bask in the pride that comes with achievement. They celebrate graduation from the prison's high school.

Despite this and other encouraging examples, programs inside prisons do not seem to reform the majority of inmates. The reason is simply that people cannot be rehabilitated unless they want to be. As John DiIulio says:

> Despite the heartening findings of Gendreau and others, the fact remains that mainly low-level offenders treated in the community are the ones who show any significant susceptibility to programs designed to rehabilitate. There is little in the latest studies to give one hope that violent, [or] repeat (two or more felony convictions), or violent repeat offenders can be rehabilitated. And . . . there is virtually nothing in these studies to enhance one's confidence in the rehabilitative efficacy of most prison- or jail-based programs. So far as the relationship between institutional programs and recidivism goes, the best bet—and the bulk of the existing evidence—remains squarely on the side of "nothing works."

A teacher in a prison education program helps two students with an assignment.

Despite the fact that programs inside prisons do not seem to rehabilitate most offenders, there is good reason to continue offering them. Programs help maintain order in prison. For example, most inmates would rather be working, attending educational classes, or receiving vocational training than sitting in their cells doing nothing. When these programs are used as rewards for good behavior, they encourage inmates to avoid violating the rules.

Rewarding good behavior

What happened at the Butner, North Carolina, Federal Correction Institution demonstrates how well this works. Butner was opened in 1976 as an experimental facility. Its inmates were hard-core offenders, but they were given a great deal of freedom to move about and interact as long as they obeyed certain rules. At the same time, they were offered a wide variety of self-help programs, such as basic education, drug rehabilitation, and group therapy, which they attended only on a voluntary basis. Then a research team was hired to study how these programs affected the inmates' recidivism rate.

A positive effect

The team found that the programs had no effect on what the inmates did after they were released. Programs did not influence recidivism or employment records. However, the team found that the programs did have a significant positive effect on the inmates' life inside Butner. Their 1987 report stated: "When inmates were allowed to volunteer for programs, they not only participated in more programs, but they also completed more programs. There were fewer disciplinary

Prisoners from a Texas correctional facility clean up a public park as part of a rehabilitation program.

problems and fewer assaults." That means programs can be an important management tool because they make inmates easier to manage.

A realistic view

The bottom line on rehabilitation seems to be that programs should be offered in prisons for the sake of better management and the few inmates who will turn their lives around because of them. However, research indicates that rehabilitation programs should be centered in the community where low-level offenders on alternate sentencing can work toward a new life free of the punishment and problems that permeate, or spread throughout, the prison environment.

Many Americans do not want to accept research results that show that their goals for prisons are at least partially unrealistic. They want prisons to "cure" crime. And they want prisons and prisoners to remain out of sight and mind while it happens. Americans are reluctant to take a realistic look at their prisons, because they do not want to see what the prisons reveal about their society. Prisons are a showcase of society's failures—abuse, neglect, poverty, discrimination, greed, lack of jobs and education, and the desire for instant gratification. They are expected to cure problems that are far beyond their reach. Thus, efficient, effective prisons are only part of the answer to America's crime problem. The rest of the answer lies in pursuing solutions to the conditions in society that contribute to the criminalization of so many citizens.

A prisoner displays the pass he has earned for good behavior. Rewards such as these give inmates incentives for keeping order and being useful.

Glossary

alternative sentence: Any one of a variety of community-based punishments imposed instead of imprisonment; also called creative sentence.

boot camp: An alternative sentence of three-to-six months of shock incarceration based on the hard work and harsh discipline of military boot, or basic training, camp.

criminalization: The process whereby the prison experience turns inmates into more hardened criminals than they were when they entered prison.

determinate sentence: A sentence of a fixed period of imprisonment imposed by a court.

deterrence: The prevention of an action, such as crime.

early release: A program in which inmates are released from prison, usually on parole, before they have completed their sentences.

emergency release: A program whereby a state gives early release to enough inmates to reduce the overcrowding in its prisons to comply with court-ordered limits.

felony: Any one of a number of crimes serious enough to warrant imprisonment.

general deterrence: The theory that the threat of punishment by imprisonment will keep people from committing crimes.

house arrest: An alternative sentence whereby offenders are imprisoned in their own houses instead of going to prison.

incarceration: Imprisonment as the result of sentencing for criminal behavior.

indeterminate sentence: A period of incarceration set by a judge that usually specifies both a minimum term that must be served and a maximum term; the offender is eligible for parole after the minimum term has been served.

individual deterrence: The theory that punishing criminals by sending them to prison will keep them from future criminal activities.

intensive probation: A probation program with strict rules, such as meeting with a probation officer every day.

judicial intervention: A ruling made by a judge that imposes conditions of prison operation on prison managers.

mandatory sentence: A sentence required by law to be imposed and enforced on certain offenders.

parole: The conditional release of inmates from prison after a portion of their sentences has been served.

penal: Having to do with punishment for crimes.

penitentiary: A prison.

penologist: An expert in penal theory.

plea bargain: A system in which felons are allowed to plead guilty to a lesser offense than the one they were arrested for in order to save the state the cost of a trial.

privatization: The building and operation of prisons for the federal or state governments by private corrections firms.

probation: An alternative sentence served under supervision in the community.

recidivism: The return to criminal activity by an offender who has been released from prison.

rehabilitation: The theory that offenders can be taught to change their behavior and become law-abiding citizens.

selective incapacitation: The theory of imprisoning mainly the limited number of offenders who commit the majority of crimes.

shock incarceration: The theory that the initial three months or so of imprisonment provide the most deterrence and that, for most offenders, longer sentences do more harm than good.

victim restitution: Financial payment made by offenders to the victims of their crimes.

work release: A program that allows inmates to attend school or work outside their place of imprisonment.

Organizations
to Contact

The following organizations provide information about prisons and the criminal justice system. Some offer opportunities for individuals to become personally involved in prison issues such as reform and legislation.

American Correctional Association (ACA)
8025 Laurel Lakes Ct.
Laurel, MD 20707
(202) 331-2260

The ACA, founded in 1870, strives to positively influence national and international correctional policies and to promote the professional development of correctional employees. It offers a variety of publications and correspondence courses on corrections and criminal justice and publishes the professional journal *Corrections Today*.

American Friends Service Committee (AFSC)
1501 Cherry St.
Philadelphia, PA 19102
(215) 241-7130

The AFSC was founded by the Religious Society of Friends (Quakers) and operates local and national criminal justice programs focusing on advocacy, education, and policy development. The national office publishes analysis and action reports. The AFSC, which attempts to relieve suffering and find nonviolent approaches to social justice, is a corecipient of the Nobel Peace Prize.

Bureau of Prisons/U.S. Department of Justice
320 First St. NW
Washington, DC 20530
(202) 514-2000

The Bureau of Prisons administers the federal prisons. It offers numerous reports, publications, and pamphlets regarding federal prisoners and the federal prison system.

Fortune Society (FS)
39 W. 19th St., 7th Floor
New York, NY 10011
(212) 206-7070

FS membership includes ex-convicts and others interested in prison reform. The society seeks to create a greater public awareness of prisons and the problems faced by convicts before, during, and after incarceration. It publishes the quarterly *Fortune News*.

The Heritage Foundation
214 Massachusetts Ave. NE
Washington, DC 20002
(202) 546-4400

The foundation is a conservative research institute dedicated to, among other things, strict prison sentencing policies. Its Heritage Resource Bank provides information on one thousand studies, and it publishes the monthly *Policy Review*.

International Association of Residential and Community Alternatives
PO Box 1987
La Crosse, WI 54602
(608) 785-0200

Association members work in community-based treatment programs for ex-offenders with the goal of helping them achieve a satisfactory return to the community. The association provides public information and education to help communities cope with crime, drug and alcohol abuse, mental health issues, delinquency, and other social problems.

National Council on Crime and Delinquency (NCCD)
685 Market St., Suite 620
San Francisco, CA 94105
(415) 896-6223

The NCCD is an independent, nonprofit organization that involves citizens in prison reform, develops alternative criminal justice methods, and conducts major research projects. Publications include the monthly *Crime and Delinquency*.

The Rand Corporation
PO Box 1019
Sacramento, CA 95812-1019
(916) 441-4214

Rand is an independent, nonprofit organization that conducts research on national security issues and the public welfare. It publishes numerous books and reports on prisons and sentencing.

The Sentencing Project (TSP)
918 F St. NW, Suite 501
Washington, DC 20004
(202) 628-0871

TSP is a national, nonprofit organization that works for sentencing reform and develops alternative sentencing programs. It offers various books and pamphlets regarding prisoners and prisoners' rights.

Suggestions for Further Reading

Renardo Barden, *Prisons*. Vero Beach, FL: The Rourke Corporation, 1991.

Frank Browning and John Gerassi, *The American Way of Crime*. New York: G.P. Putnam's Sons, 1980.

George Cadwalader, *Castaways: The Penikese Island Experiment*. Chelsea, VT: Chelsea Green Publishing Company, 1988.

Henri Charrière, *Papillon*. Translated by June P. Wilson and Walter B. Michaels. New York: William Morrow, 1970.

Phyllis Elperin Clark and Robert Lehrman, *Doing Time: A Look at Crime and Prisons*. New York: Hastings House, 1980.

Ann Kosof, *Prison Life in America*. New York: Franklin Watts, 1984.

Donald McCormick, *The Master Book of Escapes*. New York: Franklin Watts, 1975.

Lois Smith Owens and Vivian Verdell Gordon, *Think About: Prisons and the Criminal Justice System*. New York: Walker and Company, 1992.

Julie N. Tucker and Barbara Hadley Olsson, eds., *The American Prison: From the Beginning . . . A Pictorial History*. Laurel, MD: The American Correctional Association, 1983.

Ann E. Weiss, *Prisons: A System in Trouble*. Hillside, NJ: Enslow Publishers, 1988.

Tom Wicker, *A Time to Die*. New York: Quadrangle/The New York Times Book Company, 1975.

Works Consulted

Francis A. Allen, *The Decline of the Rehabilitative Ideal: Penal Policy and Social Purpose*. New Haven, CT: Yale University Press, 1981.

"American Notes: Gimme Shelter," *Time*, December 16, 1991.

David C. Anderson, *Crimes of Justice*. New York: Times Books, 1988.

David L. Bender and Bruno Leone, eds., *America's Prisons: Opposing Viewpoints*. San Diego: Greenhaven Press, Inc., 1991.

James Bennet, "Sentences That Make Sense," *The Washington Monthly*, January 1990.

Malcolm Braly, *False Starts: A Memoir of San Quentin and Other Prisons*. Boston: Little, Brown, 1976.

Janice Castro, "A Judge Whose Ideas Nearly Got Him Killed," *Time*, March 9, 1992.

Dennis Cauchon, "'Lock'em up' Policy Under Attack," *USA Today*, September 1, 1992.

Todd R. Clear and George F. Cole, *American Corrections*. Monterey, CA: Brooks/Cole, 1986.

Elliott Currie, *Confronting Crime: An American Challenge*. New York: Pantheon, 1985.

John J. DiIulio, *No Escape: The Future of American Corrections*. New York: Basic Books, 1991.

Robert Draper, "A Guard in Gangland," *Texas Monthly*, August 1991.

"The Drug Peace in California," *The Economist*, January 4, 1992.

Michel Foucault, *Discipline and Punish: The Birth of the Prison*. Translated by Alan Sheridan. New York: Pantheon, 1977.

Jack Friedman and David Lustig, "A California Prison Hopes Wild Horses Can Keep Its Inmates from Lives Spent Defying the Law," *People*, December 19, 1988.

Molly Ivins, "Small Favors: A Jewel of a Scandal," *The Progressive*, September 1991.

Tamar Jacoby, "A Web of Crime Behind Bars," *Newsweek*, October 24, 1988.

Elizabeth Kolbert, "As Inmates Pour In, Cuomo Plans 3,000 Beds in Prison Gymnasiums," *The New York Times*, June 3, 1989.

Patrick A. Langan, "America's Soaring Prison Population," *Science*, March 29, 1991.

"Lockup," *U.S. News & World Report*, October 22, 1990.

Andrew H. Malcolm, "Explosive Drug Use Creating New Underworld in Prisons," *The New York Times*, December 30, 1989.

"One in Four," *The New Republic*, March 26, 1990.

Heather Rhoads, "The New Death Row," *The Progressive*, September 1991.

Robert C. Rowland, *Behind Bars: The Problems Plaguing Our Correctional System.* Lincolnwood, IL: National Textbook Company, 1989.

"Russell Hackler's Punishment Fit the Crime and the Criminal to a T: He Made an Arresting Sight," *People*, August 27, 1990.

Michael Satchell, "The Toughest Prison in America," *U.S. News & World Report*, July 27, 1987.

Robert E. Sullivan Jr., "Reach Out and Guard Someone," *Rolling Stone*, November 29, 1990.

Scott Ticer, "The Search for Ways to Break Out of the Prison Crisis," *Business Week*, May 8, 1989.

Gail Cameron Wescott, "Squeeze You Like a Grape," *Life,* July 1988.

DeWayne Wickham, "Drug 'War' Is a Failure; Let's Call a Truce Now," *USA Today*, September 8, 1992.

Index

About the Author

Lois Warburton earned her master's degree in education at Clark University in Worcester, Massachusetts. Her previous published works include nonfiction articles, magazine columns, short stories, and poetry. In 1990 she retired from her own word processing, writing, and editing business to travel and write books. Ms. Warburton has written seven books for Lucent Books.

Picture Credits

Cover photo by Steven L. Alexander/Uniphoto Picture Agency
AP/Wide World Photos, 6, 34, 35, 42 (bottom), 51, 53, 98
Archiv Fur Kunst Und Geshichte, Berlin, 10
The Bettmann Archive, 13, 15, 16, 22, 89
California Department of Corrections, 63, 84, 85
Fritz Studio Photo, Minnesota Historical Society, 29
Grafikus, 41, 62
Hibbard Photo, Minnesota Historical Society, 30 (top)
The Mansell Collection, 12, 14, 17
Minnesota Department of Corrections, 21, 30 (bottom)
Minnesota Historical Society, 28, 31
New York State Department of Correctional Services, 27, 60
Pennsylvania Department of Corrections, 78
Reuters/Bettmann, 76
© Stock Boston, Inc., Barbara Alper, 36
© Stock Boston, Inc., Cathy Cheney, 95, 97
© Stock Boston, Inc., Bob Daemmrich, 86, 99, 100
© Stock Boston, Inc., Laima Druskis, 24, 92
© Stock Boston, Inc., Spencer Grant, 45
© Stock Boston, Inc., Steve Hansen, 38
© Stock Boston, Inc., Richard Pasley, 101
© Stock Boston, Inc., David Powers, 91
© Stock Boston, Inc., Rick Smolan, 68
© Stock Boston, Inc., David Woo, 42(top) 72
UPI/Bettmann Archive, 8, 43, 48, 54, 57, 59, 65, 66, 94
The Wackenhut Corporation, 9, 70, 81